CONCILIUM

Religion in the Eighties

CONCILIUM

Concilium 168 (8/1983): Ecumenism

MARY
IN
THE CHURCHES

Edited by
Hans Küng
and
Jürgen Moltmann

English Language Editor
Marcus Lefébure

T. & T. CLARK LTD.
Edinburgh

THE SEABURY PRESS
New York

October 1983
T. & T. Clark Ltd, 36 George Street, Edinburgh EH2 2LQ
ISBN: 0 567 30048 X

The Seabury Press, 815 Second Avenue, New York, NY 10017
ISBN: 0 8164 2448 9

Library of Congress Catalog Card No.: 82 062761

Printed in Scotland by William Blackwood & Sons Ltd, Edinburgh

Concilium: Monthly except July and August. ISSN: 0010-5236.
Subscriptions 1983: UK and Rest of the World £27·50, postage and handling included
(new subscribers £25·00); USA and Canada, all applications for subscriptions and
enquiries about *Concilium* should be addressed to The Seabury Press, 815 Second
Avenue, New York, NY 10017, USA.

CONTENTS

Editorial:
Mary in the Churches

AN ECUMENICAL issue of *Concilium* devoted to Mary: not the easiest of undertakings! Has not Mary been largely left aside in the ecumenical discussions of recent decades? 'Mary in the Churches'—surely a topic to cause embarrassment?

1. AN ECUMENICAL MARIOLOGY?

Apart from a few exceptions the evangelical churches have lost practically all interest in Mariology; Martin Luther's famous commentary on the Magnificat had more or less no lasting theological or spiritual effect; for many people, as a result of their reaction against the Catholic Church and their Christocentrism, Mariology has in fact become 'Mariolatry'—a negative symbol of ecclesial faith. *Orthodox* theology, on the other hand, has kept the classical Mariology of the ancient Church, embodying it in its liturgy and hagiography. But it is the *Catholic* Church which has heightened the figure of Mary theologically and 'used' her in the service of a particular doctrine of salvation; moreover, with the proclamation of the 1854 and 1950 dogmas, Mary has got into the ambience of papalism and triumphalism.

At the Second Vatican Council (1962-1965), however—and this was in itself a sensation—unambiguous criticism was voiced concerning certain excesses of Marianism in both theory and practice. For internal, Catholic reasons as well as for ecumenical ones John XXIII had set his face against any new dogmas. After a very emotional debate (which ultimately saw Cardinal König of Vienna opposing Cardinal Santos of Colombo), and by 1,114 votes to 1,074, the Council rejected the proposal to draw up a separate conciliar document on Mary, incorporated its presentation of her into the Constitution on the Church, and explicitly warned against Marian exaggerations.

All who took part in these conciliar debates were aware that the strained Marianism which had reached a final climax under Pius XII was now in crisis. So after the Council it was not surprising that, apart from the publications of a few specialists, theological books and articles on Mary became rarities; even in the Roman Catholic Church it looked as though the broad river of Mariology was going to dry up.

But had it always been a broad river? Even theologians are too inclined to identify 'Catholic tradition' with received ideas. Often they do not know the *Tradition*; often—as far as the *Western* and Roman tradition goes—they do not know, for instance:

that even as late as Augustine there is no mention of either hymns or prayers to Mary, nor of Marian feasts;

that not until the fifth century do we have the first example of a direct hymnic salutation of Mary ('Salve sancta parens', Caelius Sedulius);

that Mary's name was not inserted into the Roman canon until the sixth century;

that after Venantius Fortunatus the sixth century saw an increasingly rich development of Marian poetry in Latin and also in German;

that the Eastern feasts of Mary's Annunciation, 'Dormition', Birthday and Purification were not adopted in the West until the seventh century;

that the legends concerning the miraculous power of prayer to Mary do not crop up until towards the end of the tenth century. . . .

No. Devotion to Mary did not arise in the West but in the *East*, in the form of the cult of the 'Virgin for ever', the 'God-bearer' and the lofty 'Queen of Heaven':

it was here that Mary was first called upon in prayer ('Under thy protection . . .' third/fourth century) and commemorated in the liturgy;
it was here that Marian legends were first told and Marian hymns sung, and that churches were first called after her (fourth century);
it was here that Marian feasts were introduced and Marian pictures were created (fifth century);
it was here, at the Council of Ephesus in the fifth century (after a skilful political manoeuvre by Cyril of Alexander), that the Mother of Jesus was hailed as 'God-bearer' (*theotókos*). This was a new, extra-biblical title, not definitely authenticated before the preceding century, but it was enthusiastically received by the populace of this city of the 'Great Mother' (originally the Virgin Goddess Artemis, Diana), and has since become a part of the doctrinal tradition of both East and West, qualified, however, by the Council of Chalcedon (451) in the phrase: 'born of Mary the Virgin . . . according to his humanity'.

Can there be a recovery of a firmly-based (i.e., biblically-based and ecumenical) Marian devotion and theology, after the crisis of Marianism at Vatican II? This will only happen if people are prepared to face uncomfortable truths. Speaking 'as an evangelical theologian, a man and a European', *Jürgen Moltmann*, a co-director of *Concilium*'s Ecumenical Section, has clearly set forth in his opening critique the unease felt by Protestants, in view of history, about the question of Mary. He analyses what is seen as the negative side of traditional Roman Catholic Mariology (its connection with the rule of celibacy, political exploitation, the aspect of satisfying a 'religious' need), and suggests positive conditions for an *ecumenical* Mariology in the future: rooted in and guided by the biblical witness to Miriam, Mother of Jesus and member of the post-Easter community, it would be a Mariology in the service of Christology and in the context of pneumatology.

2. THE BIBLICAL ORIGINS

Even today many dogmatic theologians are unaware how meagre is the scriptural basis for a 'Mariology from above', nor do they realise how much more realistic and credible Mary becomes when understood in the socio-cultural context of her time. Here we are working for a 'Mariology from below' and this becomes very clear in the *first section* on the *biblical origins*, whether we read the article by the Jerusalem writer *Schalom Ben-Chorin* on the Mother of Jesus as seen from a Jewish viewpoint, the paper on the Marian tradition of motherhood and the Magdalene tradition of friendship by *Elisabeth Moltmann-Wendel*, the Evangelical Tübingen theologian, or finally the exegetical survey of that most experienced of American Catholic exegetes, *John McKenzie* SJ, on the Mother of Jesus in the New Testament.

McKenzie writes from the perspective of a lifetime's exegetical work, and although he does so in an unmistakable personal style and is not afraid of making his own standpoint clear, it is striking that the expository parts of his article present nothing other than the consensus of historico-critical exegesis. He is supported in this by other leading American Catholic New Testament scholars like Raymond E. Brown and

Joseph A. Fitzmyer (who, together with their evangelical colleagues Karl P. Donfried and John Reumann, have given us a remarkable ecumenical study of Mary) and by numerous European exegetes. If, arising from this exegetical consensus, we find that the Matthean and Lucan infancy narratives can only be accepted as historical in a qualified sense, that Jesus' relationship to his family and even to his mother was at best cool, that his mother was not among those at the foot of the cross and that it was Mary Magdalen who played the premier role at the resurrection, these are not the result of private opinions but emerge from the documentary evidence of the Synoptic Gospels themselves.

3. DIFFERENT TRADITIONS

In this issue we are challenging all Christian churches and theologies to reflect on their own history with a view to a better ecumenical future. This arises from the *second section* on the various ecclesial and theological *traditions*: the central problem is not so much how each distinctive tradition is to confront the contemporary intellectual climate, but how it can come to grips with its own origin—the New Testament account of Mary.

This applies just as much to *Orthodox* theology, and here the Orthodox theologian *Nikos Nissiotis* from Athens explains its position. He does this in a far-reaching way in so far as he draws out the connections between Mariology and Christology, pneumatology and ecclesiology and on this basis develops implications for a theological anthropology. The Orthodox theologian could here be speaking largely for the traditional Catholic Mariology, especially when he starts from Mary as the 'God-bearer', from the theological significance of the virgin birth, and from the typological interpretation of Mary as the 'new Eve' (which contains a critique of an all-too masculine soteriology). And the attentive reader will not fail to note that this particular Mariological conception is at odds with other theological projects in this issue in so far as these latter are more concerned with a historico-critical appropriation of the figure of Mary that appears in the New Testament.

The contribution of the Kiel church historian, the Evangelical *Gottfried Maron*, shows that *Evangelical* theology has faced the critical question, though at different times, in different churches, with varying degrees of radicality and consistency. But this leads on to the further question: Has not Evangelical theology—which at the time of Luther and of Trent can hardly be described as anti-Marian, and which only became largely anti-Marian as a result of the Catholic developments of the Counter-Reformation and the nineteenth century—cultivated an exaggerated reserve in this area, resulting in the not unjustified criticism, on the part of many women, of a theology that is all too patriarchal and a church that is all too masculine? The silence of Evangelical theology on the Marian texts of the New Testament seems to betoken neglect rather than reverence. Thus this Evangelical writer regards the new impulses from Catholic ecumenism, feminist theology and the Evangelical religious communities as a challenge to Evangelical theology and the Evangelical Church. Naturally it remains a fact that the two Marian dogmas of 1854 and 1950 are a great ecumenical obstacle.

Catholic theology no doubt finds it hardest to deal with these issues. But the Norwegian *Kari Børresen*, a Catholic woman historian and theologian, was best qualified, on the basis of her numerous studies, to outline as briefly as possible the various historical tendencies, and also to criticise a number of exaggerated developments in the Roman Catholic area. Many Catholic theologians will agree with her:

when, as against the title 'Mother of god' (*mater Dei*) which was used officially for the first time by Vatican II, she definitely prefers 'God-bearer' (*theotókos*; *Dei genitrix, Deipara*), used in a deliberately restrictive sense by the great ecumenical councils;

when she regards the typology of Mary (or the Church) as the 'New Eve' (the obedient Eve or Church as opposed to the old disobedient Eve) as obsolete, because of its androcentric framework involving the total subordination of the female element;

when, in line with the chapter on Mary in Vatican II, which is at least in principle 'minimalist', i.e., christocentric, she sees Mary in parallel, not with Christ, 'christotypically', but with the Church, 'ecclesiotypically';

when she finds the basis of the new Marian dogmas problematical. . . .

4. NEW IMPULSES

It is in fact astonishing how the figure of Mary has undergone a new interpretation today outside theology. Influences are perceptible here which often run counter to the theological and dogmatic interest in Mary; in any case theology cannot simply take them over to confirm its own position. Thus the purpose of our *third section* is to document these *new impulses*, showing how the figure of Mary can be seen in quite diverse perspectives. Here, too, the reader is left to make up his own mind.

With regard to devotion to Mary it is common knowledge that the situation of Latin America is very different from that of Europe and North America. Yet it takes someone like *Virgil Elizondo*, the Director of the Mexican-American Cultural Centre in San Antonio, Texas, a man who is at home in both traditions, to explain to Westerners how devotion to Mary—illustrated by 'Our Lady of Guadelupe' in Mexico—can be such an eloquent expression both of the plight of the Latin-American Indian and of protest against it. Elizondo speaks with refreshing frankness of things which are mostly kept silent by the Catholic hierarchy, or else overplayed (e.g., by 'kissing the ground'): the heavy guilt of the Catholic Church in Latin America for its involvement in politico-economic, sexual-patriarchal, social, psychological and also religious repression. In the face of this repression, the Marian appearance reported by an Indian signifies the start of a liberation of the silent, exploited Indian people and their greatly ill-used women from the powers oppressing them, and not least from an all too masculine and fear-inducing God/Judge. All the same an outsider cannot quite refrain from wondering whether this kind of Marian devotion (with the decentralisation of popular piety which it implies) would have been necessary at all if, right at the outset, Christian missionaries had preached, not the God of the rulers, but the Jesus of the gospels and his God (with all the attendant socio-political consequences).

Mary herself needs to be liberated from the images into which she has been forced by the masculine priestly hierarchy in particular, but often enough by women too; this becomes only too clear from the perspective of feminist theology in the article by the Dutch theologian *Catharina Halkes*, who teaches feminist theology in the Theological Faculty of the Catholic University of Nijmegen. Halkes draws a helpful distinction between Mary as a historical figure and as a (by no means to be rejected) symbolic figure, between the Mary of official doctrine and the Mary of devotion (and like Kari Børresen, Catharina Halkes is unhappy about the use of the image of Bridegroom and subordinate Bride (= Church—Mary = woman). The protest of radical feminists like the American Mary Daly is aimed at the Mary to whom theological thought fails to do justice in her authentic womanhood but only 'in relation' to the Father, the Son, the Spirit. Feminist theology aims to overcome the stereotyping of roles of men and women in the process of salvation, particularly with regard to Christ and Mary. The theology of woman and the Latin-American liberation theology joins hands here in a 'liberation Mariology', represented here by the American Catholic Rosemary Radford Ruether: in this context the 'Fiat' can be understood as creative receptivity and the 'Magnificat' as a prophetic song of freedom.

Catharina Halkes's plea for a historically constructive approach to the figure of Mary, which must also draw upon depth-psychology, is carried forward by the observations on Mary and the human psyche by the Münster theologian *Maria Kassel*. In this article Mary is not seen simply as the biblical figure of the historical mother of Jesus, but as the reflection of deeply-rooted psychic states of a universally human kind: Mary as the archetype in the sense of Jungian psychology. First Kassel turns her attention to the traditional form of Marian devotion, which from a psychological point of view fulfilled positive functions ('Mary' the archetype as the presence in the Church of the feminine and the unconscious), but also decidedly questionable ones (by splitting the feminine archetype into two and projecting all the negative, 'seductive', Eve-attributes on to real women, reserving the good aspects for Mary, the exemplar). Looking to the future, it may be possible—after a period of abstinence—for the archetype 'Mary' to reveal its potential, under certain conditions, for helping men and women to become more completely human, in the sense of a new unity of masculine and feminine, conscious and unconscious, animus and anima. In this way the masculine psyche could be liberated from the compulsion to project its unconscious fear of the feminine on to real women; the excessively masculine Church could dismantle its fixation on the topic of sexuality, and woman could become man's partner within the Church's institutions.

The last contribution to this issue, by *Karl-Josef Kuschel*, germanist and theologian at the University of Tübingen, reveals for the first time the astonishing and hitherto largely unknown influence of the figure of Mary in the work of modern German-speaking authors, from Brecht and Hesse to Günter Grass, Heinrich Böll and Luise Rinser. Untrammelled by theological and Church interests, these authors are able to confront Marian traditions with their origins ('poor Mary' and 'Mary on the side of the poor'), parody the linguistic stereotypes and social clichés connected with her, outline a utopian picture of Mary which is critical of power-structures, look for secular transfigurations of the Marian image; they can create their own, personally-tinged mythology, nourished on Indian philosophy or Jungian psychology, or discover in Mary today—often on the basis of a political, utopian interpretation of the 'Magnificat'—a figure in the history of feminine emancipation and of political liberation. The combination of myth and politics, critique and utopianism are characteristic of a picture of Mary in contemporary literature; frequently it is based, spiritually, on the 'Marian dialectic' of power and powerlessness, defeat and victory.

So it seems to me that we really have an ecumenical Marian issue, written by Catholics, Orthodox and Evangelicals from both sides of the Atlantic, men and women of various disciplines. There will be no lack of material for discussion! The Editors sincerely hope that there will be a fair and unemotional discussion. Naturally each of our authors is only responsible for his own contribution. Let the arguments alone, from whichever side, prove decisive!

We should be clear on one thing right from the start: far from trying to evaporate or even nullify the significance of Mary for theology, the Church and the history of spirituality, this ecumenical issue aims to provide a new interpretation of the figure of Mary for our time, freeing it of clichés and rigidities and thus smoothing the path for a *genuinely ecumenical picture of Mary*, the Mother of Jesus, so that *all* Christian churches can once again discover the truth of Luke's words: 'All generations will call me blessed.'

HANS KÜNG

Translated by Graham Harrison

Editorial:
Can there be an Ecumenical Mariology?

AN ECUMENICAL dialogue about Mariology, if it is carried on in all sincerity, with a readiness to understand the deeper roots both of Marian devotion and of the resistance to it, is bound to be difficult. That is why Mariology has been largely excluded from the official ecumenical dialogue. Where Mariological conversations did occur, they often resulted in a mere consensus of specialists, which was of no great importance to the churches represented. If we want to see what an ecumenically compelling Mariology would look like, we must dig deeper and be prepared to face the anti-ecumenical factors at work in Mariology as cultivated by the Church.

Confronted with the grievous history of Church divisions and of the persecution of Christians by Christians, a history graven on the memories of those who suffered from it, it sounds a little naïve when the Bishop of Osnabrück suggests making Mary the 'Patroness of Ecumenism' (quite apart from the incongruity of *patron*age in the case of a woman). Looking back into history we are bound to notice that Marian devotion and its corresponding Mariology have had a divisive rather than a unitive effect: did not the Church's veneration of the 'Mother of God' seal the final separation of Christianity from Judaism, for what had the 'goddess and her hero' to do with the Jewish mother Miriam (Schalom Ben-Chorin)?—The discrepancy between Church teaching and the New Testament is nowhere as great as in Mariology. One need only compare Jesus' apparently historical valediction to his mother (Mark 3:31-35 par) with Church statues of the Madonna and Child.—Did not the Church wage war against the Albigensians, Cathari and Waldensians (reform movements based on a return to the Bible) under the sign of the Virgin?—And during the political Counter-Reformation, how many evangelical churches were forcibly changed from 'Christchurches' to 'Mary' churches, the Crucified Saviour on the cross behind the altar replaced by the statue of Mary and the Child?—And what about the counter-revolutionary conservatism of the Roman Catholic Church in its fight against the Enlightenment and autonomy, democracy and modern science, religious freedom and the critique of religion—was not this too under the sign of belief in Mary? The new Roman Catholic Marian dogmas of 1854 and 1950, too, are part of the context of this 'anti-Modernism'.—Many have seen in the Marian appearances of *Fatima* a religious, apocalyptic response to the Bolshevist revolution in Russia. Occasionally we may see the modern feminist movements re-vamping the old Mariology, but we are not misled into thinking that the patriarchal and celibate mother-images can now be utilised in the liberation of woman from her humiliation by the masculine world. Mariology, we must say in all honesty and objectivity, has so far been anti- rather than pro-ecumenical. The more the Marian superstructure has been developed, the more it has estranged Christians from Jews, the Church from the New Testament, Evangelical from Catholic Christians, and Christians in general from modern man. But is the Madonna of Church Mariology identical with Miriam, the Jewish mother of Jesus? Can we find Miriam in the Madonna? Or, because of all the splits and divisions that have been perpetrated by the churches in her name, perhaps we *ought* to go back and find out about her? No doubt the ecumenical movement can leave Mariology aside and get on with other and perhaps more important topics. But to do that is to fail to deal with the past. The danger then is that the past will eventually repeat itself.

Of course, this is not the time to be developing an 'ecumenical Mariology'. All the same we can try to envisage the conditions under which such a thing may come about. By 'ecumenical' I mean (1) the Christian community of the separated churches, (2) the biblical *oikoumene* of Christians and Jews, (3) the secular community formed by Christians together with the whole 'inhabited earth', i.e., first of all with all the poor, for whom the earth is still not habitable. And here let me make a personal comment: I am conscious of thinking as an Evangelical theologian, as a man, and as a European. That is my starting point: not, I hope, my prejudice.

1. NEGATIVE CONDITIONS FOR AN ECUMENICAL MARIOLOGY

By 'negative conditions' we mean those interests and functions in Mariology which hinder ecumenism by not allowing Mary to appear as a figure in the liberating history of the gospel of Christ. I will just mention a few which strike me particularly as an Evangelical theologian. No doubt there are others.

(*a*) The close connection between *Mariology and celibacy* strikes everyone who finds both equally foreign to him. Does the celibate consecrate himself to a virginity which he reveres in the divine Virgin? Does she become a wife-substitute, as Ludwig Feuerbach suspected? Does the celibate's own physical mother remain for him the exemplary woman, with the result that, far from him outgrowing his mother-attachments, they are religiously reinforced? Is it right for the Church to allow and encourage such inhibitions? Does it not stimulate masculine fantasies in which the woman is the saint or the great sinner, but never a real human person? Since Jesus' call to discipleship there has always been a free-will celibacy. But it is part of the community of the new messianic life centred on Jesus: 'Whoever does the will of God is my brother, and sister, and mother' (Mark 3:35). It is a limited renunciation for the sake of an unlimited gain. It is not a renunciation requiring religious compensation. Evidently, the messianic community of those who follow Jesus is strong enough to break the power of family origins. Thus Jesus turns his mother, brother and sisters away, bids them farewell. This messianic community, however, is open to all believers, including Jesus' mother and family, not because of their blood relationship but because of their faith. That is why Mary and the brothers of Jesus appear in the Easter community (Acts 1:14): as believers. Mary's relationship is more that of a sister. This being so, we are in a better position to see *Jesus' friendship* with the women who accompany him, in the first place with Mary Magdalen (E. Moltmann-Wendel). This open friendship seems to have played a much bigger role in the messianic community than the mother-son relationship which became the focus in later Mariology and stamped its influence on the Church. Does not celibacy make the Church symbolically the mother and the believers the Church's children? What happens to the horizontal relationships which are essential in every family, brotherly, sisterly, and friendly relationships? Any future ecumenical Mariology should be developed, not in connection with a celibate priestly hierarchy, but with regard to the kind of community intended by Jesus, i.e., a community of faith bound together by open friendship.

(*b*) Hitherto a *political Mariology* has hindered the development of an ecumenical Mariology. We have already indicated the fateful significance of traditional Mariology in the Counter-Reformation, anti-Modernist and counter-revolutionary movements. No doubt what we have here is an emotionally deep-seated and in part justified aversion to an increasingly masculine Christianity and political world. But at the same time one has to recognise the Church's fear of the Christian's coming of age, of man's moral autonomy and of the sovereignty of the people—fears which have found their expression in the modern flowering of Marian devotion and the modern Marian dogmas. Probably, however, the real politicising of Mariology is to be found in *Marian apocalyptic*: Rev. 12 speaks of a 'woman clothed with the sun, with the moon under her feet, and on her head a crown of twelve stars'. In great pain she bears a child. But the 'red dragon' tries to get hold of the child to devour it, and persecutes both woman and child. There follows the final battle between the dragon and those who have the testimony of Christ. Although this woman is not called Mary but probably signifies the Israel of God and the Church, this 'final drama' has had a deep influence on the Christian Marian imagination: Mary seated on the crescent moon, Mary clothed with the sun, Mary with the twelve-starred crown—this is the apocalyptic Mary. The proto-gospel of Gen. 3:15 was also applied to her, so that pictures and statues show her, and not her Son, treading on the serpent's head. In this way Mary became the Madonna-guardian of all believers persecuted by the red dragon, the Conqueror (Victrix) in the apocalyptic final battle of the world. Modern Mariology is also to be seen in the context of this apocalyptic interpretation of our time as the 'end-time'. I hold this apocalyptic Mariology to be just as baneful as the *apocalyptic friend/foe attitude* and the expectation of Armageddon. In any case dragons can change their colours: they are not always 'red'; there are others.

(c) Finally, Marian devotion has always been a melting-pot of the most diverse *religious needs and desires*. Since the Gospel of Christ did not grow out of a popular religion but called into being a messianic community from all peoples, the Church in the various countries took up the local folk religion and adapted itself to it. Yet through ecclesial symbol and ritual the Gospel of Christ was to remain the critical standard for religious needs and their satisfaction. This process of adaptation and critical corrective is particularly clear in the history of Mariology. For the most part the manifold forms of Marian devotion far exceed what is officially acceptable to the Church. Thus the problem as such is whether and how far theology can adopt these religious wishes and wish-fulfilments without losing its Christian identity. Mariology must not become the market-place of depth-psychological speculations. More pointedly: how Christian is Marian popular piety and how Christian is the Church's Mariology? Evangelical theologians have always been at a loss when, in order to justify the new Mariological dogmas, tradition and, more recently, the *sensus fidelium* were adduced along with and going beyond Scripture. They were afraid that this development spelt the end of truly Christian criteria. On the other hand one has to recognise that the Protestant attachment to the principle of Scripture was not based solely on faith in 'Christ alone': it was also conditioned by the repression of the religious dimension in modern industrial society. This raises the question of the religious relevance of Christian faith. A future ecumenical Mariology will arise in the field of tension between Christology and folk religion. In doing so, as Virgil Elizondo has shown, it will become a 'Mariology from below' in which the oppressed people will achieve freedom and dignity in the gospel, the gospel of Christ.

2. POSITIVE CONDITIONS FOR AN ECUMENICAL MARIOLOGY

Only with great reluctance am I prepared to say what seem to me to be the positive pre-conditions for an ecumenical Mariology, for ecumenical unity concerning them has yet to be reached, and it is by no means certain.

(a) The source and standard for the Church's Mariology is to be found in the biblical witness to Miriam, the mother of Jesus, a member of the original Christian post-Easter community

Ecclesial Marian devotion and ecclesial Mariology must present the figure of the real

Mary without any distortions. In order to see the real Mary, the whole biblical witness needs to be taken into account. It will not do to construct a history of biblical tradition in order, on the basis of it, to arrive at speculative Mariological extrapolations. This would be merely a retrospective justification of the Church's alienation from its real origin. Thus it is no good taking Luke's figure of Mary in the Infancy Narratives on the one hand and then scarcely paying any attention to the disturbing accounts in the Synoptics concerning Mary's encounter with Jesus and her absence from the group of women beneath the cross. Nor is it good to ignore the relationship of Jesus to his mother, as many Evangelical Christologies do. An exemplary study which points the way forward for ecumenical Mariology is the 'Gemeinschaftsstudie von protestantischen und römisch-katholischen Gelehrten': *Maria im Neuen Testament. Eine ökumenische Untersuchung* ed. R. E. Brown, K. P. Donfried, J. A. Fitzmyer, J. Reumann (Stuttgart 1981).

(*b*) **Mariology must serve Christology; it must neither detract from it nor become emancipated from it**

Like John the Baptist, who is often depicted with her at the foot of the cross, Mary points away from herself and towards her Son; her whole meaning is to be found in this self-forgetting and Christological gesture. A christocentric Mariology would also do justice to the significance of Christ for Mary, revealing her as the real Miriam. However, this would mean that the other images of Mary, the image of Wisdom (Prov. 8), the image of the Woman of the Apocalypse (Rev. 12), the image of the great Goddess, the Queen of Heaven or the Eternal Feminine must give way, allowing Mary to be seen once again in the context of the other women around Jesus—among whom Mary Magdalen is particularly prominent. In a christocentric Mariology Mary is an essential figure in the liberating Gospel of Christ, and not the image of regressive dreams or apocalyptic fears. That is the real meaning of the truism, 'No Mary without Christ, no Mariology without Christology'.

(*c*) **A biblically-based and christocentric Mariology will express the presence and activity of the Holy Spirit in the destiny of Christ and of Christians**

According to the gospels the activity of the Holy Spirit prior to Easter was directed solely to Jesus (John 7:39). It is the Risen One who sends the Spirit to the community. With one exception: according to Luke 1:35 Mary conceives by the Holy Spirit and is filled with the Holy Spirit. She is the first person to play a part in the history of the Holy Spirit, as determined by Christ. Thus wherever the Holy Spirit is spoken of, Mary too will be mentioned, and where Mary is referred to theologically, the Holy Spirit is involved. But there must be no confusion: it is not Mary, but the Holy Spirit who is the source of life, the Mother of believers, the Wisdom of God and the indwelling of the divine mystery in creation which will renew the face of the earth. Mary bears witness to the presence of the Holy Spirit. Far from making the divine Trinity into a Quaternity, she is a sign of the Trinity's openness for the unification and the eternal life of the whole creation.

JÜRGEN MOLTMANN

Translated by Graham Harrison

PART I

Biblical Origins

B

John McKenzie

The Mother of Jesus in the
New Testament

THE SCOPE of this article is to review the place of Mary in *contemporary biblical studies within the Roman Catholic Church*. One must first notice that biblical studies about Mary, like Mariology as a whole, have come to a nearly complete halt since Vatican II. Other articles in this collection will treat of this 'Marian silence'; I shall try to state as well as I can the factors which have arrested biblical studies, as well as the responsibility of biblical studies for the present eclipse of Mariology.

1. A RECENT ECUMENICAL DISCUSSION

My task has been rendered much easier by the publication of an ecumenical set of papers on Mary in the New Testament (= MNT), produced by the scholars who were members of the *Lutheran-Roman Catholic ecumenical dialogue* sponsored by the Lutheran and Roman Catholic churches *in the United States* since the conclusion of Vatican II.[1] This group has produced some other ecumenical discussions of theology. The Marian studies, like the other works, are models of theological discussion; they are based on solid learning, they are open and judicious, they are free from sectarian narrowness and passion, and their conclusions are cautious and candid. Had such discussions been possible 450 years ago, the Protestant Reformation need not have happened. I do not know how many of my readers will think this would have been a good thing. Certainly the discussions establish a set of new relations between the separated Churches. Could I fulfil my commitment by doing no more than referring to this work, I might do something better than what I shall do.

This book shows that the representatives of the churches concerned in the discussions agree that the New Testament is to be interpreted according to the principles and methods of historical-critical interpretation. This will be news to a number of Catholics and Protestants alike, how many I cannot determine. The results of these methods show that *the amount of positive information we have about Mary is extremely small*. To Catholics this could be alarming, if it were left at that; we shall briefly mention some of the long cherished beliefs which have been deprived of any basis in historical reality.

2. CRITICISM AND MARIAN TRADITIONS

In this essay, as in MNT, the discourse is concerned entirely with the *New Testament as a theological and historical source*. We are not concerned with the value of tradition, however one interprets the word. But it would be idle to pretend ignorance of the fact that the historical-critical method of investigation is no kinder to tradition than it is to the New Testament; we shall illustrate this by a few examples. The New Testament affords *no historical basis for the beliefs in the immaculate conception or the assumption* of Mary; the base in tradition for these beliefs is another question. The New Testament affords *no basis for belief in Mary as the mediatrix of all grace*. When I studied theology nearly fifty years ago, my professor said that this belief was ripe for dogmatic definition; now it has fallen into the Marian silence.

Criticism has not supported the traditional names of Joachim and Anna as the parents of Mary, nor such liturgical commemorations as the presentation of Mary in the temple. Criticism has shown that the *Protevangelium Jacobi*, which is the source of these beliefs, is devoid of any historical value. In addition, most of the apocryphal gospels are not only removed too far in time and in place from the events to establish themselves as historical sources, most of them are not free of at least traits of heresy. The heresies concerned are docetism, which denied the reality of the humanity of Jesus, and gnosticism; the bizarre variety of forms in which gnosticism defies summary, but let us venture the statement that these forms expressed a belief in dualism.

3. THE INFANCY NARRATIVES OF MATTHEW AND LUKE

Mary appears most prominently in the gospels of Matthew and Luke; this is due to the presence in both of the infancy narratives (Matthew 1-2 and Luke 1-2). The absence of any trace of these narratives in Mark and John, as well as in the rest of the New Testament, is best explained by the assumption that *Mark, John, Paul and the other New Testament writers had never heard of any infancy narratives*; other explanations are regarded not only by the authors of MNT but by most scholars as contrived.

It is only from the infancy narratives that the name of *Joseph*, the husband of Mary, is derived, except for three appearances as the patronymic of Jesus (Luke 4:22; John 1:46, 6:42). There is no question that Mary had a husband (except from some ancient rabbinical slanders not taken seriously) and that he had a name, nor does the material in the other New Testament books demand the mention of his name. The idea occurs, but is by no means demanded, that its absence is due to a lack of information.

The infancy narratives of *Matthew and Luke are the only sources for the virginal conception of Jesus* (meaning without a human father), the name of Joseph as the husband of Mary and the legal father of Jesus, and the birth of Jesus at Bethlehem. We have already mentioned the rarity of the appearances of the name of Joseph. The same is true of the birth at *Bethlehem*, elsewhere unattested; in the New Testament Jesus is called Jesus of *Nazareth*. Matthew appeals to a quite unhistorical crime of Herod to move Jesus to Bethlehem from Nazareth, and Luke appeals to a quite unhistorical census to move Joseph and Mary from Nazareth to Bethlehem for the birth of Jesus. There are problems involved in the place of the birth of Jesus, but they do not touch the examination of the Mariology of the gospels; they do touch the *historical credibility* of the infancy narratives. It is not rash to ask how much information Matthew and Luke had about the birth of Jesus.

An ancient and devout belief of Christians represented Luke, stylus and tablet in hand, sitting at the feet of Mary writing down the memories of her old age. With all reverence one may ask at whose feet Matthew sat; outside of the points of accord mentioned above, the two narratives differ entirely in details, and *the differences* are not trivial; they *are irreconcilable*. This suggests some caution in dealing with the points of agreement, one of which is pertinent to Mariology, the virginal conception.

The authors of MNT point out that *Matthew 2 and Luke 2, read without the respective preceding chapters, would never lead to the conclusion of a virginal conception*. If, as we have been suggesting, neither Matthew nor Luke was dealing with any one who had had personal and immediate experience of the events, then they must have dealt with assorted memories of assorted value collected from assorted sources—unless one prefers to suppose that each wrote from his own independent imagination, unfettered by any information whatsoever. I suppose most readers will find this assumption untenable. Hence I believe I may suppose that the birth narratives of Matthew and Luke (their respective chapters 2), already recognised as quite independent of each other, contain no reference to the virginal conception found in their respective chapters 1, which are independent of each other and of their respective chapters 2. I trust readers will understand that the importance of the material justifies entering into such detail.

4. THE VIRGINAL CONCEPTION OF JESUS

It also justifies further investigation of the historical reality of the virginal conception of Jesus. This investigation has been made by Joseph Fitzmyer and Raymond Brown.[2] Certainly *the virginal conception of Jesus is not on the same historical level as the death of Jesus on the cross*. The cautious conclusion of Brown is that historical and critical analysis of the texts does not exclude an affirmation of faith that Jesus was virginally conceived. The equally cautious conclusion of Fitzmyer expresses concern that the texts should not be made to say more than they say. Neither of these scholars, both of whom were members of the ecumenical team which prepared MNT, suggests that the literary evidence compels an affirmation of faith of the virginal conception of Jesus.

Nor does either scholar exclude the theory that the *virginal conception* is present in the text *as a theologumenon*, an expression through narrative of the belief that Jesus is the son of God, accepted by some recent Roman Catholic scholars.[3] This view seems to be supported by the fact that the belief that Jesus was the son of God is certainly expressed frequently in the New Testament, especially in the gospels and in Paul, *without any appeal to the absence of a human father*. This is most remarkable in the gospel of John, whose proclamation of the Only-Begotten fits admirably with the announcement of the virginal conception. Yet John shows no awareness of the virginal conception. One may sum up the literary evidence for the virginal conception by saying that no witnesses of the virginal conception could have been adduced except Mary and Joseph; the gospels of Matthew and Luke not only show no evidence of the testimony of Mary and Joseph, but have positive indications that they were written without their testimony.

5. THE PERPETUAL VIRGINITY OF MARY

The question of the perpetual virginity of Mary, defined traditionally as *ante, in et post partum* (before, during and after birth), is not strictly speaking a biblical question. Yet there is some biblical material which must be considered for some aspects of the question. The gospels show no evidence of parturition without loss of virginity: this would be the virgin birth in the strictest sense of the term. The other New Testament books are equally silent concerning *virginitas in partu*. Evidence to support the truth of this belief must be derived from other theological sources.

The question of the perpetual virginity of Mary *after the birth of Jesus* (*virginitas post partum*) certainly falls within the sphere of exegesis; it depends on the identity of the brothers and sisters of Jesus, mentioned several times in all four gospels and in Acts. There is no question that the word 'brother' is often used in the Bible to designate other members of a kinship group beyond those who are children of at least one common parent; it designates members of the same clan, tribe or even nation. In the New Testament Christians are designated as brothers 160 times, and Jesus is quoted as saying that one who does his father's will is his mother and brother (Matthew 12:50; Luke 8:21; Mark 3:35 adds 'sister').

But the use of 'sister' to designate more remote kinswomen is much rarer. And there is no instance of the use of 'brothers' and 'sisters' for more remote kinsmen and kinswomen when the words accompany an enumeration of names.[4] James is hardly called 'the brother of the Lord' because he was thought to do the will of the father. Of him and of Joses, Judas and Simon (Mark 6:13) *the more probable meaning* (and of the sisters mentioned *ibid.*) *is children of at least one common parent*; and so it would be understood for any one else. In the same context of Mark the one parent mentioned is Mary; this does not support the explanation sometimes advanced that they are children of Joseph by a previous marriage. One may wish that the evangelists or their sources had spoken with greater precision of the family relations involved; since they did not, careful interpretation obliges us to *leave the texts in their imprecision*.

6. JESUS AND HIS FAMILY

(a) Exegetical Facts

Related to the question of the perpetual virginity of Mary is the question of the *personal relations* between Jesus and the members of his 'family', whatever the degree of kinship may have been. James, 'the brother of the Lord', appears in Acts as a leading member of the Jerusalem community. But all other references to the 'brothers and sisters' of Jesus explicitly indicate some *coldness* in the relations between them and Jesus or imply it; in the hypothesis that the coldness clearly shown in the text of Mark has been glossed over by Matthew and Luke, their editorial treatment of the material has left a picture which is neutral at best.

Unbelief and hostility would be clearly seen in Mark 3:21 & 3:31-35 if any one else but Jesus and possibly his mother were involved; Matthew (12:46-50) and Luke (8:19-21), who preserve the saying of Mark 3:31-35, seem to blunt its sharpness. Their omission of Mark 3:21 speaks for their understanding of this verse. The exchange between Jesus and his 'brothers' in John 7:1-9 does not depend on the other gospels; but independently or not, John says that the brothers of Jesus did not believe in him (7:5).

The presence of Mary with the brothers of Jesus in Mark 3:21 & 31-35 does not show that she shared their sentiments. Decisions in such family problems were made by the adult males of the extended family. With this reservation, one may ask whether the personal experience of Jesus with his kin may have added some sharpness to his *harsh words about detachment from the members of one's immediate family* (Matthew 10:34-37; Luke 15:26). This is not to imply that these texts are quotations of the exact words of Jesus; the problem of how they arose is no greater and no smaller than it is for other words attributed to Jesus. Jews had a very strong sense of family and blood kinship, a sense found in all cultures except the fragmented societies of highly developed civilisations. Perhaps no more than this is needed to explain the saying; it may be gratuitous to wonder whether the saying implies anything about the relations of Jesus with his own immediate family. But we are safe in assuming that *the gospels do not suggest warm relations*.

(b) Problems of theological evaluation

The arguments for *the perpetual virginity of Mary* are all drawn from what used to be called the *ratio theologicae convenientiae* (arguments of theological propriety). In Mariology this type of argument was summed up in a saying attributed to Duns Scotus: *Deus potuit, decuit, igitur fecit* (God could have done it, he should have done it, therefore he did it).[5] How much validity contemporary theologians attach to this principle I do not know. It certainly seems to make *human judgment of what it is proper for God* to do rather than reported actual events the standard of what happened in history.

Since the alleged evidence for the perpetual virginity of Mary is not such as to *withstand normal historical investigation*, one understands why early and later believers substituted theological propriety for the missing evidence. It was easy to assume that the human vessel which served to bear the Incarnate Word should have been used exclusively for him and shared with no other, either before or after. It is less easy to assume that the vessel should have been preserved undamaged; for this *implies a hidden supposition that parturition 'damages' the feminine organs of reproduction*. This in turn leads to a further suggestion that it is 'better' that these organs never be used for their biological and social purposes.

At this point the student begins to sense the possible influence of some form of *gnosticism*; and he does not have to appeal to *ratio theologicae convenientiae* to know that in early Christianity there were forms of gnosticism which identified sexuality with sin and radical sinfulness. One knows that the belief that Mary conceived Jesus without what was for centuries called 'the stain of carnal commerce' suits gnostic ideals, as does the belief that the highest fulfilment of femininity is the combination of motherhood and virginity. One may conclude that *a belief which has such dubious associations demands more evidence than the assumption that the conception and birth of Jesus were other than normal human processes*. The wonder of his birth, if one believes of him what Christians have always believed, is more wonderful if he was born exactly like any other son of woman. These considerations make us ask whether the ancient arguments from theological propriety speak to us with their former urgency.

Further questions arise when the belief in the virgin birth is compared with some other beliefs which were judged heretical even in the early Church. There were several varieties of the error called *docetism*, which in several ways denied the genuine full humanity of Jesus. It may be stretching a point to say that orthodox belief has had more trouble in preserving the affirmation of the humanity of Jesus than in preserving the affirmation of his divinity.

The particular form of docetism to which I refer was the belief that Jesus passed through the body of Mary as through a tube or a canal. Ancient *ignorance of the processes of fetal growth* allowed believers to fail to see that this belief denied to Jesus the normal processes by which one becomes a fully developed human being; *effectively, they said that Mary was not the mother of Jesus*. Perhaps we must ask whether to deny Jesus a human father is also to deny him the normal and 'natural' development of a human individual; without a human father, was Jesus human? One may ask whether the virgin birth is not a part of an ancient worldview which is as much out of date as the clear biblical belief in a geocentric universe.

7. MARY AND JESUS: MOTHER AND SON

The question of the personal relations of Jesus to his mother, arrogant as such a discussion may appear to be, cannot be passed over. I say arrogant, because such matters of personal intimacy may be none of our business. Even for men and women of historical interest whose lives are much better documented than the lives of Jesus and Mary these are questions which usually fall out of the historian's view.

The few personal exchanges of Jesus and Mary which are reported in *the gospels tell us little*; these are the words at the finding in the temple (Luke 2:48-49), the words at the wedding at Cana (John 2:3-5) and the words of Jesus on the cross (John 19:26-27). In addition there is the passage about the mother and brothers of Jesus previously discussed, to which we shall briefly return. Of the passage of Luke and the two of John it may be said at once that modern scholarship is not only sure that they do not represent the actual words spoken, it is not even sure that the words represent anything ever spoken by Jesus and Mary.

Hence the unquestioned *brusqueness of the words of Jesus* in the temple and at Cana tell us nothing except what an early Christian writer imagined about the way Jesus might speak to his mother—or any Jewish man might speak to his mother. The words of Jesus on the cross we shall take up below. We have already seen that the words of Jesus to and about his brothers exhibit no cordiality. The question is whether *Mary*, who accompanied the brothers in the episodes mentioned, is *included in the coldness of Jesus towards his family*.

Certainly the response of Jesus to his family (Mark 3:33-35) makes no distinction between mother and brothers, nor does the anecdote express any dissociation of Mary from the brothers expressed by Mary or by any one else. If any one else were concerned, the anecdote would be read as showing *passive co-operation of Mary with the action of the brothers*. Perhaps we should leave it there, and abandon further explanation to those who believe without any biblical evidence except for Luke's annunciation story that the faith of Mary in her son was always firm and clear from the moment of his conception.

8. MARY AS IDEAL DISCIPLE

The words addressed to Mary from the cross (John 19:26-27) have no parallel in the synoptics; the other gospels do not even mention the presence of Mary at the cross, although they mention the presence of other women (Mark 15:40-41; Matthew 27:55-56; Luke 23:49). The evangelists say clearly that all the disciples had fled and were absent from the death of Jesus; it is not strange that the sources of the gospels were ambiguous on who was actually present, but the synoptics are not ambiguous on the absence of Mary.

It seems that *we must accept the words of Jesus to Mary and the beloved disciple as a theological construction of John*. The authors of MNT interpret this as presenting Mary as the ideal disciple. In Mark and Matthew Mary does not appear as a disciple. In Luke's gospel she does not so appear, but the two references to her thoughtful recollection of events (Luke 2:19, 51) may indicate the beginnings of discipleship. In Acts 1:14 she appears in the company of the disciples who receive the Holy Spirit. In John she is expressly committed to the care of the disciples (taking the beloved disciple as representative). I am not as sure as the authors of MNT that this presents her as the ideal disciple; *but it certainly presents the disciples as taking the place of Jesus in relation to the only widowed mother*. They become in still another sense his 'brothers'.

9. MARY AS SINLESS

This leads to the question of the biblical evidence for the *sinlessness* of Mary. The dogma of the immaculate conception of Mary was proclaimed *without any biblical evidence* and thus falls outside our scope. The same may be said concerning the belief in her sinlessness. It is true that she is not described as a sinner; neither is she described as an example of virtue. We simply do not know enough about her to assume that *any more than that she was a normally good woman*, subject to the faults and frailties of our fallen human nature; she might still be with these 'our tainted nature's solitary boast', as Wordsworth called her. Traditional belief would not even allow her growth in faith, mentioned above, which seems to show some imperfection.

10. THE REAL MARY AND THE FICTIONAL MARY

The real or the historical Mary is at least as elusive as the real or the historical Jesus, and not quite for the same reasons. The genuine historical evidence about Mary is so slight as to impose upon the historian, were any one else concerned, an embarrassed silence. We know as little about her as we know about the mother of Abraham Lincoln, about whom Lincoln is credited with a remark that all he had he owed to his angel mother. Jesus did not even say for the record that much about Mary. But this has left the imagination of Christian devotion entirely unrestrained by information.

The Mary of Christian legend, art, poetry, hymnody and even theology is a fictitious character. I am not sure that we can say of her that the Mary of faith is as important as the Mary of history. *Faith in the Mary of traditional Christian devotion is faith in something which is not true.* The symbolism of art has indeed its value; for years I exchanged Christmas cards with friends because the cards expressed my feelings about Christmas better than I could myself. The symbolism presupposes a faith in some reality which is symbolised. But what is the reality which the art, hymns and legends of traditional Marian devotion expressed?

There is no doubt that fictional characters which signify *certain symbolic values have often been deeply meaningful*; one has to think only of some of the great character figures portrayed in the works of Homer, Shakespeare and Dickens. Those whose native language is other than English will think of others.

The significance of such characters has depended on the insight, the imagination and the literary artistry of their creators. The significance of *historical characters* and events is entirely independent of any such factors; it *depends on their reality*. I would never say that the significance of Jesus depends on the insight, imagination and literary art of the evangelists, nor do I think my colleagues would. Matthew, Mark, Luke and John lack almost totally the literary and artistic genius possessed by Homer (whoever he or they was or were), Shakespeare and Dickens. *As a fictitious character Mary is entirely undistinguished. The Mary of traditional devotion is a plastic figure.* This figure seems to have met the needs of the ages which created her, and these were mostly the centuries from the tenth to the seventeenth.

One may venture a bit farther and assert that these were the needs felt by the ruling classes of Christendom which patronised the art and the literature of those centuries. The mere reality of a first-century Palestinian village housewife obviously met none of these devotional needs, because that is not what the poems, hymns, art and legends represented. About Palestinian housewives they knew nothing; if they had, they would have found her like the maids of their palace kitchens or the peasant women of their domains. They were not going to hang pictures of these humble common folk on their walls, or sing hymns praising their beauty and virtue. Before they could venerate Mary, they had to make her one of themselves; that is, they had to destroy her. We should not forget that this is the background against which she was seen to portray the ideal woman: beautiful, sinless, achieving the impossible fulfilment of both virginity and motherhood, and always a gentlewoman, 'our Lady'.

11. THE FUTURE OF MARIOLOGY

One wonders why Mariology and Marian devotion have come nearly to a *standstill since the Second Vatican Council*; the last great effort of Mariology was the declaration of the Assumption of Mary by Pius XII in 1950. Why this high tide was followed immediately by an ebb of Mariology should be an intresting theological topic to be discussed elsewhere in this symposium. But it is not entirely outside my topic to present a few speculations on the future course of developments of Mariology; and these will be affected deeply by the present silence which has fallen upon Mariology.

We have noticed that the meagre historical knowledge about the real Mary was no obstacle to the development of Mariology and Marian devotion; what Christians did not find they created. No doubt historical and biblical criticism had an iconoclastic effect upon Mariology. I raise the question whether the collapse of Mariology is to be attributed solely to the hammers of the critics. The Mary of traditional devotion was thought to meet the needs of the centuries in which she was created and flourished.

One asks whether she will meet or can ever be hoped to meet the needs of modern devotion—whether the beautiful, sinless gentlewoman who achieved the impossible fulfilment of uniting virginity and motherhood is not as much of a dodo as Saints Philomena, Christopher and Valentine. *If devotion to Mary is to revive, it must take an entirely new form.* If I knew what that form should be, I could do no better theological service at the end of my career than to say it.

As far as I can pretend to understand it, the contemporary movement of feminism can have no room for devotion to the traditional Mary. *If a new Mariology is to be formed, it will be formed by women.* There are certainly enough articulate feminist theologians to tell us what a new Marian cult should be if they wish it. If they do not wish it, it is foolish to think that male theologians can create it. It is, I believe, wrong to think that Jesus because of his gender belongs more properly to men on the assumption that we are better able by endowment to understand him. It should be equally wrong to think that for the same reason Mary because of her gender belongs more properly to women. I would like to share the hope which Paul expressed—rather vainly, so far in Christian history—that we might become just people in Christ Jesus (Galatians 3:28). But since I expect to live out my days without seeing the hope of Paul fulfilled, a respect for reality demands that for some time to come we leave Mary in the hands of her sisters. I do not know whether she will be in better hands than in the hands of men; obviously women think so, and the men who created the plaster doll of the traditional Mary should not hesitate to step aside.

I began this piece with the intention of concluding with a paragraph which I have now decided not to write. Instead, let me now conclude by saying that Roman Catholic theology desperately needs a kind of blood transfusion simply in order to assure its survival, and in time some recovery of its strength. These thoughts on Mariology have made me newly aware that we have never needed to look far into the future. Our help is ready to hand in that half of the Church which has been theologically inarticulate for so many centuries. I recommend to my colleagues that they do what I believe I have always tried to do, to assess the work of my fellow theologians not on any such trivia as creed, religious affiliation, ecclesiastical orders or dignities, academic degrees or honours or posts, nation, language, age, or gender, but simply on the persuasion of their arguments.

Notes

1. *Mary in The New Testament* edited by Raymond E. Brown, Karl P. Donfried, Joseph A. Fitzmyer, John Reumann (Philadelphia and New York 1978). Hereafter referred to as MNT.

2. Raymond E. Brown *The Birth of the Messiah* (Garden City, New York 1977); Joseph A. Fitzmyer 'The Virginal Conception of Jesus in the New Testament' in *To Advance the Gospel* (New York 1981) pp. 41-78.

3. Fitzmyer, in the article cited in note 2, at pp. 45, 66 cites R. Pesch, J. Michl and O. Knoch.

4. W. Bauer *Wörterbuch zum NT* (Berlin 1958), *s. v.*; Brown-Driver-Briggs *Hebrew-English Lexicon* (Oxford 1953), *s. v.*; Köhler-Baumgartner *Lexicon VT* (Leiden 1953), *s. v.*

5. I cannot trace the quotation as I remember it after thirty-five years. But a more recent work quotes Scotus as enumerating a principle of Mariology: 'We can with probability attribute to Mary all that has the greatest perfection, provided it is not opposed to the authority of the Church or the Scriptures' (quoted in the *New Catholic Encyclopedia* (4, 1105) from *In 3. Sent.*, 3.1).

Schalom Ben-Chorin

A Jewish View of the Mother of Jesus

'I see thee, Mary, in a thousand ways
So beautifully expressed,
But no image can express the way
In which my soul can see thee.'

(trs T. L. W.)

THUS WROTE the German romantic poet Novalis (ps. for Friedrich von Hardenberg, 1772-1801) in his famous *Mariengedicht*.

Mary has indeed been represented in many ways but not as the *young oriental Jewish mother* which she originally was. But this is the way in which I, as a Jewish author writing from Jerusalem, saw her, and this is how I will try to convey this image to Christian readers.

1. MARY AS A JEWISH WOMAN

This simple outline of Mirjam (Mary) the mother of Jesus, however, should not obscure the radiant image which the faithful have of the Queen of Heaven but simply remind us of her real existence on this earth in the midst of all the spiritual elaboration.

'As for Mary, she treasured all these things and pondered them in her heart' (Luke 2:19, 51).

This remark shows Mary's situation and her nature. We should see her in our imagination as an oriental, Jewish girl, about sixteen years old, who is obviously exposed to some extraordinary commotions the meaning of which is beyond the understanding of a barely adolescent mother.

There was nothing out of the ordinary in the fact that she became a mother at such a young age in the Jewish situation of that time: it was then, and remained still until quite recently, quite common in oriental-Jewish circles. It was only in the modern State of Israel that the law put the marital age at eighteen, and among Yemenite Jews this met with total incomprehension.

As was always the way in this tradition, we have to see Mary as completely passive with regard to this situation. Her maternal instincts were roused, she looked after the infant, had no opinion about the actual events, but remembered and wondered about what was extraordinary in so far as it could be grasped at all.

So we have to see Mary as busying herself about the house. A large family, a small income. We know from the last section of *Proverbs* (31:24) that the ideal Hebrew woman was not only concerned about the home and the family. She also contributed to the upkeep and the livelihood: 'She makes them linen garments and sells them; she delivers girdles to the merchant' (Proverbs 31:24).

In other words, the accomplished woman, praised in this alphabetic poem which the Jewish father recites on Friday evening at the beginning of the Sabbath at supper in praise of woman, produces various things, particularly by weaving, and sells the produce of this home industry. Her value is therefore recognised without reservation: 'Her children rise up and call her blessed; her husband also, and he praises her: many women have done excellently, but you surpass them all' (Proverbs 31:28-29).

But none of all this appears in Mary's life. She is the *Mater dolorosa*, the mother burdened with sorrow. Her first-born son praises her nowhere; he rather addresses her with a certain harshness: 'O woman, what have you to do with me?' (John 2:4). Nor do we hear of any compliments on the part of Joseph, merely that he had his suspicions about her.

We also have to see the *religious life* of a Jewish woman as rather *introverted* in those days. In the outer world her religious life is far less apparent than that of the male. While the woman is also bound by the commandments, she is dispensed from all such commandments as are tied up with definite times. The reason for this is that she is tied to her duties as a mother. Since the mother had to keep the children quiet for long periods on end, she could not keep up with the hours prescribed for prayer, so she was dispensed from those. And the woman was naturally dispensed from the most comprehensive of all duties, the study of the Torah.

2. THE FAMILY

We must think of Mary's family as that of a simple and obviously *needy manual labourer*, but this should not be interpreted as primitive. The New Testament contains two didactic epistles, one from James and one from Judas, which are attributed to Jesus' brothers. (James was even considered later on as the head of the original community.) These epistles show the high cultural level of both brothers. Even if, from the point of view of critical research, we cannot accept James and Judas as the exclusive authors of these letters without qualification, tradition has it that these brothers of Jesus were fully capable of writing these letters. Since we cannot accuse the gospel's reportage about the family of Jesus of any idealising tendencies, we have to take this tradition seriously.

The *lack of understanding* of the brothers and the mother is no secret. The relatively late conversion of the mother and the brothers to accepting Jesus is well known. When, therefore, such an epistolary tradition could persist in spite of all these realistic facts, we have to accept that the lately converted brothers give the impression of being educated men. And whilst this clearly applies strictly only to James and Judas, it seems reasonable to conclude that Joseph and Mary provided their children, especially the sons, with a broad education.

But in the past as today we should certainly distinguish the position of a woman in a large town, here Jerusalem, and in a small provincial town like Nazareth. The circle of Scriptural scholars and the surroundings of the Temple gave women a place in the learned discussions of the wise men. This may well have been different in the countryside, but from the meagre references to Mary's life we may infer that she was constantly in *contact with Jerusalem*. Family ties linked her, on the one hand, with the

Levites and, on the other, with the dynasty of David, if we follow the indication of the gospels.

The noble origin of a family which has since been reduced to poverty may well have ensured a higher level of culture. It has often been observed that in impoverished aristocratic circles people keep up a certain cultural standard which no longer corresponds to their actual social situation.

So we have the impression of a family belonging to an impoverished landed gentry who in their environment live by the demands of a *higher spiritual sensibility* which is rather beyond those of their locality. Although we should not exaggerate this situation it nevertheless produced the atmosphere which Jesus breathed in the first years of his life.

The New Testament tells us *nothing about a possible teacher* Jesus may have had. It is true that there is a Talmudic tradition which mentions such a teacher but, as I tried to show in my book *Bruder Jesus*, this has no historical-biographical value.

It is much more natural to accept that Joseph himself educated his son, and even before him Mary, since, up to the age of five, children were cared for by their mother. No mother endowed with a fair amount of elementary knowledge would fail to impart this to her child. Without this kind of initial education of the child Jeschua, the episode of the twelve-year-old Jesus in the temple of Jerusalem (Luke 2:41-50) would become completely unintelligible. No doubt, this story aims at presenting Jesus as a kind of child prodigy, but even a prodigy presupposes a certain amount of formation.

An analysis of the parables of Jesus gives the impression that for him the *love of the father* was *decisive* while the love of the mother plays no part whatever. This love of the father without doubt implies a transposition to the heavenly Father, God. There seem to be two ways of interpreting this. Jesus may have wanted to transcend the fatherly love of Joseph which he had experienced in his early years. But, personally, I prefer another interpretation: Jesus wanted to idealise a fatherly love he longed for but never had. This longing contrasted with the painful experience which he must have had with his uncomprehending mother.

3. THE FAMILY CONFLICT

If there is one feature in Jesus' character which stands out in its clarity, it is the anti-family attitude which only accepts relationship by choice, not by the ties of kinship.

This alone must already have been a profound shock for his mother and brothers, and they may well have agreed with those hostile critics of Jesus who said: 'He has an unclean spirit' (Mark 3:30).

This remark immediately precedes the episode reported by Mark about the failure to bring Jesus back home (Mark 3:31-35).

His mother and brothers were standing outside, in front of the house (was it Jesus' house?). It is not clear whether they would not go in or could not because the house was besieged by supporters or the merely inquisitive.

A messenger, perhaps a child which can more easily slip through the crowd, managed to come close to Jesus and told him that his mother and brothers had arrived. The mother was explicitly mentioned first. This was with good reason: it refers to one of the ten commandments: 'Honour your father and your mother'. The Jews take the command to honour one's parents very seriously, which is not the case where brothers and sisters are concerned. Both the Law and the custom required that Jesus should get up at once and meet his mother. This is why the mother is properly mentioned first here.

But he disowns her. And he does so in a way which is characteristic of a Jewish dialogue, and answers in the form of a question: 'Who is my mother? . . . and who are my brothers?' (Sisters are not even mentioned.)

Such an attitude would be considered scandalous in any society, but among Jews it would even be more strongly resented.

The power of family ties among the Jews is proverbial and this is underlined in what may well be the oldest layer of the Jewish ritual. Within the family the father had a kind of priestly function. It was the father who led the domestic worship, not in opposition to but rather as complementing the Temple worship. The children are blessed by father and mother. The father has the duty, which he cannot simply pass on to some teacher, but must hand on to his son, namely that of preserving the heritage of tradition: 'You shall teach them diligently to your children' (Deut. 6:7). 'And you shall tell your son on the day (of the Passover)' (Exodus 13:8). Thus the family became also a kind of sacred community which gathered, for instance, round the paschal lamb in order to consume it as a cultural family meal.

Father, mother and children are therefore not only a natural unit, but also *a cultural and sacred one*. It lies at the root of the *berith*, the covenant which was concluded with Abraham as head of his family, and so of the tribe.

This enhanced concept of the family must be understood to grasp the full tragic effect provoked by Jesus' disowning the unity of the family which God had established. . . .

This decisive scene should be linked with that where a deeply moved woman listener sang his praise and Jesus' cold rejection: 'As he said this, a woman in the crowd raised her voice and said to him: "Blessed is the womb that bore you, and the breasts that you sucked!" But he said: "Blessed rather are those who hear the Word of God and keep it." (Luke 1:27-28).

I feel quite justified in quoting this passage because it fits into the problem I am trying to discuss. Even the admirers, obviously mainly women, saw the great rabbi they were wholly devoted to as the son of a clearly blessed mother. Could any woman in Israel hope to play a higher part than that of being the mother of such a son, who teaches with authority, who can dominate demons, can heal the sick and even raise the dead to life? Any woman in Israel would, in times of hardship and oppression, dream of becoming the mother of the promised saviour. Was this promise not fulfilled for this particular mother, at least partly?

With a woman's solidarity, the woman in the crowd does not explicitly praise Jesus himself but his mother, the body which bore this child and the breast that gave suck to the infant.

Jesus, however, did not intend to share with his mother something of the revelation which he disclosed to the people in his conduct and his person. He had nothing in common with her. She clearly had never understood him, thought him somewhat deranged and accepted him too late. He would not allow any intimacy. He firmly deflected any praise of his mother. 'Still happier those who hear the Word of God and keep it', and at this moment this statement and this situation are meant to cover both the mother and the brothers.

4. MOTHER AND SON

The mother's position is different from that of the other members of the family. She does not believe in the son either. But what does that mean? A mother, especially a Jewish mother, may well not believe in her son at the level of her conventional consciousness, so profoundly influenced by her social environment, and yet still do so at the deeper level of the subconscious. Mind and heart, especially a mother's heart, do not go hand in hand. This son must have caused her a lot of pain. He broke through the structure of family life as it was locally accepted and practised. He roams around through the country and creates unrest. He does things that are dangerous: danger threatens from the Jewish authorities and from the hated occupying power of the Romans. He puts *the whole family at risk*.

Would she not often have seen him as that ill-bred son, described in the law as not listening to his father and mother, rebellious and moreover a wastrel and a drunkard? The law lays down that he should be brought before the elders of the town to be condemned and stoned so as to banish this evil from Israel (Deut. 21:18-21).

The tradition of the Talmud has linked this *Ben Sorer u More* with such impossible conditions, so wildly exaggerated, that this harsh law could never be put into practice. But probably this was wholly unnecessary since Deuteronomy literally lays down that father and mother should hand their son over to the tribunal. Where would one find a mother willing to do that? But he who curses father and mother is also liable to the death penalty according to the law, and this law, too, remained more defunct than the words in which it was prescribed.

From the little we know about Mary's attitude towards her grown-up son we can only conclude that it was *full of tensions*.

5. UNDER THE CROSS

And now we come to that extraordinary adoption scene where the son, dying on the cross, once again addressed his mother so strangely as 'woman', abandoned her and, with a nod in the direction of the disciple, said to her: 'There is your son'. He then turned to the disciple and said: 'There is your mother'.

It would be easier to understand this scene if Mary had been left behind as a lonesome widow without children, but this is far from the case: she had sons and daughters. The present scene simply shows that Jesus had given up *all contact with his brothers and sisters*. However far apart he and his mother might be, he did not want to leave her in the company and care of these brothers and sisters, especially as she had not left him in the hour of his martyrdom. So he asked the disciple to look after her and in this way tried to inaugurate a new mother-and-son relationship.

At this same time he used the expression 'woman' again when addressing the last of the Marys present under the cross, Mary of Magdala. The remarkable adoption scene implies the distancing of himself from his mother, but even so this 'distancing' is very different from his attitude towards his hostile brothers and sisters who are simply by-passed. The text only adds that from this hour the disciple, obviously John, looked after the mother of his master. Nothing is said about Mary's reaction to all this: in the usual oriental way she remained *completely passive*.

Translated by T. L. Westow

Note

This contribution by Schalom Ben-Chorin, a Jewish author living in Jerusalem, is an extract from his book *Mutter Mirjam. Maria in jüdischer Sicht* (Deutscher Taschenbuchverlag, Munich, No. 1784). A fair number of books have been written by Jews about Jesus. But if one excepts Schalom Asch's novel about Mary, which appeared over twenty years ago, Schalom Ben-Chorin's book is the only Jewish work which has tackled this subject.

The Jewish view of Mary as seen by Ben-Chorin (who calls her *Mutter Mirjam*—mother Miriam) is based on New Testament sources as well as on Jewish sources, which may not mention Mary explicitly but elucidate the life of a Jewish woman at the time of Herod's Temple.

Elisabeth Moltmann-Wendel

Motherhood or Friendship

1. TWO BIBLICAL TRADITIONS ABOUT WOMEN

THE ATTENTIVE reader of the Bible will be continually struck by the firm way in which the Church's tradition has put Mary, the mother of Jesus, in the foreground while pushing Mary Magdalene, the first proclaimer of the resurrection message, to the back of the stage. The tradition about Mary, the mother of Jesus, is fed largely by Luke's gospel. But we find the tradition about Mary Magdalene in all four gospels; and it is the tradition about the women which is best attested, and from the most unified standpoint.

(a) Mary Magdalene the first witness of the resurrection

Mary Magdalene is witness to the very beginning of the resurrection message. The gospels differ only about the circumstances. In Mark, Mary Magdalene is accompanied by Mary, the mother of James, and Salome. In Matthew, her companion is 'the other Mary'. In Luke, too, we are told about another Mary, as well as Joanna and other women. In John and in the late closing passage of Mark she is alone. The character of the charge she is given varies too. In Luke and in the late final passage of Mark she tells the disciples only what she has experienced, while in Mark and Matthew she and the other women are charged by the angel to proclaim to the disciples what they have heard. In John she is given this charge by the risen Jesus himself.

These are not chance variations. They are different emphases given by the individual evangelists to the story about the women. Luke tells of no special charge, and there the group of disciples is already viewed as an élite, celibate community which the group of women serves,[1] and in which Mary Magdalene's function is restricted too. Her presence at the cross is not explicitly mentioned either, though this is reported by the three other gospels. Nor is there any mention of her presence at the tomb, to which Mark and Matthew refer. Luke puts the story of her call, as the healing of a daemonic sickness, in the same context as the call to other women, thereby neutralising its unique character.

In spite of these differences, the picture of Mary Magdalene remains the self-contained portrait of a particular woman. As we have it, it is in striking contrast to the clashes and conflicts of the picture which the four evangelists give us in their varying picture of the mother of Jesus, who was favoured by the Church's tradition.

(b) The mother of Jesus as antitype

Mark brings out all the sharpness of the conflict between mother and son, which was probably based on historical fact. Matthew tempers this by leaving out the family's suspicion that Jesus was mad (Mark 3:20, 21).[2] Luke softens Jesus' hard saying that only the person who does the will of God belongs to the eschatological family, mitigating it by presenting Mary, in the nativity and childhood stories he includes in his gospel, as the obedient handmaid who fulfils these demands (1:38).

But the gospel of John does not carry through this picture of the believing, obedient Mary. It is true that John puts her at the foot of the cross (unlike the other traditions, which only know about the group of women associated with Mary Magdalene). He does so in order to make her the mother of the beloved disciple, who represents the ideal picture of the believing Christian. But 'because of her imperfect faith in Cana' she cannot be compared with the Lucan Mary.

So we can see that the picture of Mary in the New Testament is a conflicting one; and the two main themes of later Mariology—the virgin birth and the presence under the cross—are clearly later in origin. Yet these two themes penetrated deep into devotional practice with the help of *pietàs* and nativity scenes. All the same, the 'uprating' of Mary in Luke and John was not able to push out Mary Magdalene entirely. For she is associated with the very centre of Christian faith: the resurrection.

(c) The repression of the friendship tradition

None the less, we can already see in Luke that there was a tendency to minimise Mary Magdalene's uniqueness in favour of the group of women. The original tradition has come down to us in Mark particularly. This tells us that, unlike the disciples, who were in love with success, the women were the real followers of Jesus: it is they who perceive the messianic secret, and it is they who serve Jesus as he himself came to serve, and to give his life. This tradition is now joined by another, which stresses feminine obedience and motherliness, but still favours the group of male disciples.

Our ideas have been moulded by the theology of the mainstream churches, and we are too little informed about heretical theologies, especially their conceptions about women. This means that we have lost our eye for the two different traditions about women which can already be found in the New Testament. I should like to call these *the tradition of friendship* and *the tradition of motherhood*. The first of these traditions made itself felt particularly in the Christian traditions of protest. The second has been mainly cultivated in the mainstream Church. Even though the term 'Jesus' friend' is seldom applied to a woman—although the middle ages and the nineteenth century were two periods which were especially creative in their view of friendship: the friends of God and romantic friendship[3]—yet the fact itself has remained clear throughout the centuries: Jesus was on terms of intimate friendship with women. The two differing relationships put their stamp both on notions about women and on the picture of Jesus himself.

2. DISTORTIONS

In the first centuries of the Church's life, both traditions were able to go on existing side by side, unhindered and with equal validity. Mary was one saint among others. But when, at the Council of Ephesus, the Church decided in favour of Mary as *theotókos*, thereby picking up an image of popular piety, it pressed all ideas about women into the same mould. Consequently the friendship traditions were increasingly pushed aside. Jesus' women friends found no entry into the creed. Mary Magdalene remained illegitimate. Like the 'three Marys', the women lost themselves in local cults; or they forfeited their biblical background and fell into line among the growing army of martyrs and saints. But above all we can see the original figures changing into the images required by the anxieties and needs of a male society.

Mary Magdalene is the most fatal and typical example, and it is one which has affected the Christian idea of women down to the present day. Her story (Luke 8) was fused with the story of the woman 'who was a sinner' (Luke 7). Her flask of ointment also let her be identified with Mary of Bethany, who anointed Jesus (John 12). So in the churches of the West, three independent women turned into a monster and model of sin and grace. As Karl Künstel points out, this development goes back to Augustine especially: 'Because she (Mary Magdalene) had once been bound by fetters of sensuality' and had been a consolation to him.[4]

The figure of Martha underwent a parallel development. According to the gospel of John, she is the person strong in faith (Bultmann). She prompted the raising of Lazarus and her confession of Christ must for some Christian communities have had a meaning like the confession of Peter. She was turned into the active but less valuable housewife. She was then even typified, with her sister Mary (Magdalene): Martha became the *vita activa*, Mary the *vita passiva*; Martha the Jewish Church, Mary the gentile Church; and so on. The figures of the women were robbed of their originality and distorted; and it was in this form that they put their impress on the history of art and culture. The Mary-Martha antithesis is 'the undisputed possession of medieval spiritual writings'.[5] We already find it in Origen, later in Augustine, Gregory the Great, Cassian, the monastic Fathers Norbert of Xanten and Bernard of Clairvaux, and elsewhere.

During the flowering of medieval theology the biblical women lost their original significance. They were touched up, distorted or typified. We can compare this with the way goddesses were patriarchalised: research into matriarchy today detects this process in the prolonged transition from matriarchy to patriarchy: female figures lost their original independence, one aspect was isolated, and they forfeited their universality.[6] Artemis ceases to be the triple pre-Olympian goddess and becomes the virgin; Aphrodite becomes a whore, and Hera Zeus's matronly housewife. In the same way the biblical women were also drawn into the age-old patriarchal pattern of male fantasies. Their real historical role in Jesus' history was smothered under the feminine stereotype into which they were forced. Even the mother of Jesus did not escape, although in her case other ways emerged of integrating undercurrents of popular piety.

Even when the Reformation turned back to the gospels, this brought no change. Luther did not follow the enlightened Faber Stapulensis, who again separated the three different people Mary Magdalene, Mary of Bethany and the woman who was a sinner, pointing to the fatal error that had crept in. For Luther, Mary Magdalene remained the sinner; and in accordance with Calvin's notions of morality, the women who followed Jesus were 'of ill repute'. Martha was the person whose works were to be made 'as nothing'. The women were models for a new theology of justification. They were images of sin and grace; while their history, their relationship to Jesus, and their function at the resurrection remained undiscovered. The alteration in the Roman breviary of 1970 did at least put an official end to the fatal Magdalene tradition.[7]

3. FRIENDSHIP

We are used to thinking and working in the concepts and ideas of the literature belonging to the mainstream churches; and we have also, without knowing it, internalised many patriarchal notions about women. As a result, the tradition of friendship, of a spontaneous, free human relationship, tied to no fixed conceptions about a particular order, has been suppressed, falsified and forgotten. But in spite of everything it runs like a scarlet thread through the whole of Christian history, the history of the sects, the history of new social and religious awakenings, the history of women. It became an infection whenever women broke out of the usual order of things, or had to break out of it, and where new social possibilities opened up for them.

(a) The Magdalene tradition

In the rest of the present essay I shall confine myself to the Magdalene tradition, although the unknown Martha sub-culture especially, in its different way, throws a classic light on the undersurface of history.[8]

In the early Christian congregations, where women held office in many places, Mary Magdalene was reverenced more than Mary, the Mother of Jesus, as Jesus' intimate friend and the one he loved more than all the disciples. Unencumbered by betrayal like Peter, she represented an immediate relationship to Jesus and his message which was unequalled. She was the vehicle of revelation and could even (in the gospel of Philip) become Wisdom, 'the woman who knows the universe'.

We see the same thing in the Cathar movement in twelfth-century France: Mary Magdalene becomes the model of steadfastness, whereas Jesus' mother recedes noticeably into the background. As Gottfried Koch remarks, 'The veneration of Mary has little to do with recognition of the woman's equal role in the Church.'[9] In the women's movement which was part of the Cathar movement, Mary Magdalene as she is found in the New Testament came to life once more. In the medieval *Golden Legend* of Jacobus de Voragine, we are told that Jesus 'enflamed her entirely with love of him', and that people were enchanted by 'the sweetness of her discourse and the beauty of her countenance'. In succeeding centuries this picture of Mary Magdalene lived on in art. She is the beautiful preacher who is to be seen on medieval pulpits; in a stained-glass window in Chalons-sur-Marne she even baptises; and on an altar triptych in Lübeck she makes her brother Lazarus a bishop.[10] We know from isolated statements made by the Fathers that, in spite of all the patriarchal changes to which her image was subjected, she was still called 'the apostle of apostles'. But the breadth of this sub-culture only becomes clear when we look at the rich visual material which has not hitherto been taken seriously theologically.

(b) Modern traces of the Magdalene tradition

The Reformers, and consequently the major Protestant churches, showed no interest in this tradition. The female models that accorded with their ideals were the matrons and mothers of the Bible, like Sarah and Rebecca. But the Magdalene tradition revived again in the Protestant movements of succeeding centuries. When women became more self-sufficient, Mary Magdalene became the model which an independent reading of the Bible made available to them; whereas it was only in isolated cases that increased reverence was paid to Mary, the mother of Jesus.

Katharina Zell, the wife of the Strassburg Reformer, spoke a public valediction over her husband on his death, excusing herself for this 'scandal' on the grounds that she was acting like Mary Magdalene, though adding that 'she had no thought of being an apostle'—a rider significant of her theological tradition.[11] But in the following century (1676) the Quaker Margaret Fell already based her claim that women had a right to speak in the Church on the forgotten figures, 'the three Marys', Joanna and Mary Magdalene: They passed on the message, she said; . . . how else should the disciples have known it since they were not there?[12] The black Methodist Javena Lee deduced the right of women to preach from this central resurrection message of the Christian faith which was entrusted to a woman.[13]

In the changing churches and societies of the nineteenth century, the women who endured to the end with Jesus became paradigms for women's own social struggle. Taking the pattern of the women surrounding Mary Magdalene, women overcame their feminine role-fixation and discovered anew the first Christian charge given to the women: the task to witness to the resurrection and a changed world. In all social revolutions women found an identification here and preserved this special tradition.

But even the male theologians of the Protestant churches supported the change in the role of women which was beginning to make itself felt in the free churches. The Quaker John Rogers, for example, called Mary Magdalene 'the first preacher of the resurrection'. As a defence against Catholic Mariology and in support of a new Protestant typology, George Fox even altered the symbolic pattern which had been generally accepted ever since Irenaeus, changing the Eve-Mary typology to an Eve-Magdalene one: 'So when Christ was risen, the woman that was first in the transgression, the woman went first to declare the Resurrection out of death, out of the grave.'[14] Luther had already placed Mary Magdalene above the mother of Jesus as the prototype of greater sin and hence of greater grace. But now attempts were made to get away fundamentally from the concept of Mother Church and its images.

(c) The topical force of the Magdalene figure

Yet the apostle Mary Magdalene played no official part in the ordination debate carried on in major Protestant churches in the twentieth century. Only outsiders like Elisabeth Malo have drawn on her.[15] In the 1975 Vatican declaration her role was again played down: the women were merely supposed to prepare the apostles to become the official witnesses of the resurrection. Up to now the friendship tradition has had no theological legitimation.

Catholic women theologians have meanwhile recognised that the mother tradition is unduly one-dimensional. Elisabeth Gössmann sees that it was Mary Magdalene's task 'to witness to the faith in Christ which transforms time'. For Elisabeth Schüssler, her significance is that she helps women to find 'the meaning of their discipleship and the whole discipleship of the church'.[16] Rosemary Ruether, finally, believes that the symbol of Mother Mary has overshadowed the friend and disciple who was the first to accept the faith in the resurrection on which the Church rests.[17]

Apart from the claim it makes to the apostolate of women, the friendship tradition has theological and ethical claims too. It broke with—and will always break with—the idea of Jesus as an aloof master. Instead it stresses the mutuality and partnership of God and man. We find this in the gnostic fantasies about a marriage between Mary Magdalene and Jesus, and in the 'groupie' idea of the rock opera *Jesus Christ Superstar*; and it is repeated in Heinrich Böll's demand that the Church acquire Mary Magdalene's tenderness. Today these are desires of vital importance, which can no longer be satisfied by the domesticated sexuality of the mother cult of a Church which has been afraid of sexuality for almost 2,000 years. Friendship as Hegel understood it, friendship as 'the concrete concept of freedom',[18] embodies the hope for new human relationships of the kind we find illustrated in the forgotten New Testament tradition about Jesus' friendship with women, and its subsequent suppressed sub-culture.

Friendship was the constitutive mark of the eschatological community of the disciples. As the imminent expectation of the eschatological End-time retreated, archaic myths of origin were taken up. This was the source of the Church's Mariology. Early on, Mary, the ancient Mother Earth, met religious needs—later the needs of the Church—today the needs of depth psychology. But she cannot provide what continually breaks through in the person of Mary Magdalene, in the New Testament and in traditions of protest: that the promise of life was given to a woman friend of Jesus, and that this divine friendship is the model for faith and for a messianic community of women and men.

Translated by Margaret Kohl

Notes

1. Elisabeth Schüssler-Fiorenza *The Twelve. Women Priests* (New York 1977) p. 119.

2. See here and for the following *Maria im Neuen Testament. Eine ökumenische Untersuchung* (Stuttgart 1981).

3. E.g., Jacobus de Voragine, '. . . he took her to be his special friend', *Die legenda aurea* (Heidelberg 1979) p. 472; Meister Eckehart, '. . . the dear Martha and with her all God's friends . . .'. *Deutsche Predigten und Traktate* (Munich 1977) p. 285.

4. Karl Künstle *Ikonografie der christlichen Kunst* (Freiburg 1926) p. 427; Hans Hansel *Die Maria-Magdalena-Legende* (Bottrop 1937).

5. Matthias Bernards *Speculum virginum* (Cologne 1955) p. 194f.

6. Heide Göttner-Abendroth *Die Göttin und ihr Heros* (Munich 1980) p. 32.

7. Elisabeth Moltmann *The Women around Jesus*, Eng. trans. (London 1982).

8. *Ibid.*

9. Gottfried Koch *Frauenfrage und Ketzertum im Mittelalter* (Berlin 1962) p. 100.

10. E. and J. Moltmann *Humanity in God* (New York 1983).

11. *Religion and Sexism* ed. Rosemary Radford Ruether (New York 1979) p. 179ff.

12. Joyce L. Irwin *Womanhood in Radical Protestantism 1525-1675* (New York 1979) p. 179ff.

13. *Women and Religion in America* ed. Rosemary Radford Ruether (San Francisco 1981) p. 214.

14. *Early Quaker Writings 1650-1700* ed. H. Barbour (Grand Rapids 1973) p. 505.

15. *Frau und Religion. Gotteserfahrungen im Patriarchat* ed. Elisabeth Moltmann (Frankfurt 1983) p. 87ff.

16. Elisabeth Schüssler *Der vergessene Partner* (Düsseldorf 1964) p. 126f.

17. Rosemary Radford Ruether *Mary: the Feminine Face of the Church* (London 1979) pp. 73-74.

18. Jürgen Moltmann *The Church in the Power of the Spirit* (London 1977) p. 115f.

PART II

Various Traditions

Nikos Nissiotis

Mary in Orthodox Theology

THERE IS *no Christian theology without continuous reference to the person and role of the Virgin Mary in the history of salvation.* On this biblically and ecclesiologically justified statement have developed several trends in Christian theology. From a maximalistic approach which has created a separate chapter of 'Mariology', because of the great significance of Mary at the centre of Church life and popular piety, to the other extreme of complete silence, contemporary theology betrays a strange attitude, which can be explained as a result of long ages of polemical discussion between *Roman Catholicism and Reformation.*

On the other hand, Eastern Orthodox theology does not refer sufficiently to this topic, because Mary has been always regarded as the centre of Church worship and piety as well as of personal and communal spirituality, thus limiting theological systematic reflection to rare and occasional references to the person of the Mother of God. This is mainly due to the fact that Mariology is situated at another level, more existential, experiential and vocational than the other topics of theology. When everything in Church life speaks of and indicates Mary, including the structure of daily worship through a glorious worship and iconography, scholastic theology becomes superfluous or recognises that it is inadequate to deal with such a paramount event of immediate existential sharing of the faithful.

Without wishing entirely to justify this attitude, because one should also criticise systematic theology for being unable to handle this vital issue because of its onesidedness as a scholastic discipline dealing too much with rational approaches and definitions of the mystery of faith, we should interpret this limited reference of Orthodox theology as a sign of pious respect for a central focus of personal edification and profound liturgical experience.

This *limited reference on the part of the Orthodox Church*, however, becomes all the more conspicuous for its absence when interest in Mariology is stirred up in contemporary theological research, and especially when it serves ecumenical co-operation in theology, anthropology and the contemporary witness of the churches in modern society. This is the main reason why I have agreed to participate in this symposium of *Concilium* by way of a delayed and modest correction of the silence I have kept until now towards this essential topic of a Christian theology and of an acknowledgment of the usual absence of reference to Mariology and in worship in ecumenical circles due to an exaggerated concern not to create yet one more factor of separation and not to cause a scandal to the conscience of colleagues and brothers of other Christian traditions.

By maintaining this silence, we must confess as Orthodox that we have neglected to use one of the most genuine and representative characteristics of the ancient Eastern tradition at the service of unity, spirituality and the building of an authentic ecumenical fellowship in joy, doxology and thanksgiving. The humility and repentance that should be the fruit of a consistent reference to Mary according to our tradition enables us to realise the negative power and schlerotic nature of Church structures. An ecumenically oriented theology that does not make reference to Mariology is a crippled, anthropocentric and individualistic theological reflection. This is because it is unable to penetrate dynamically hearts and minds seeking unity in Christ through the One Spirit on the basis of a full ecclesiological approach. Reference to Mary makes theology take seriously into consideration the biblical and kerygmatic witness of the Church regarding the interpenetration of the divine and human elements in full reciprocity and unbroken co-belongingness.

1. THEOTÓKOS AND PANHAGIA

The ancient quarrel concerning the exact titles of the Virgin Maria itself reveals something of special importance for today's theological-ecumenical debate. The Orthodox use these two titles abundantly in almost an exclusive way in order to secure her *right place in the divine economy and within the Church community*.

The two terms point to the fundamental truth that one can think, speak and write about or one can meditate, worship and pray with Mary at the centre of the Church community only when one thinks of her always in inseparable unity with the Christ-event in the Spirit and the ecclesial gathering as communion of saints and the sanctified people of God. The glory of Mary is a reflected one on account of the event of the *incarnation* in which she operates not as a mere instrument for giving the carnal-fleshly embodiment to the Logos of God but as a fully involved because a distinctive and elect person, sharing in the operation of giving birth to the hypostasis of the Logos as the unique personal revelation of God in history. *'Panhagia'* (All-Holy) denotes, on the other hand, her solidarity with sanctified humanity, i.e., with all of the members of the Body of Christ when they recognise in her not simply their symbolic representation, but when they share in her holiness given by the Spirit who incarnates in the *Theotókos* the Logos of God.

The terms *'Theotókos'* and *'Panhagia'*, in other words, do not allow an easy separation of Mary from the people of God and her elevation in the sphere of heavenly glory alone as the crowned Madonna. They do not permit any reductionism of her central place in Christology, ecclesiology and especially of her solidarity with the community struggling for sanctification and restoration into the full humanity through the sole grace of Christ, operated by the Spirit. Consequently, in the Orthodox hymnology and iconography, Mary is always praised or presented with Christ and at the centre of the saints as a *representation of the worshipping and praying community*. She is always the Mother-of-God together with the incarnate Word as well as the centre of the intercessory prayers of the gathered community as the person who represents its striving towards personal sharing in the holiness operated by the Spirit in the Church.

(a) Mariology in Christology

It follows, therefore, that the word about Mary (Mariology) should not become a separate chapter of systematic theology. What the term *'Theotókos'* signified right after the defeat of Nestorianism is that *Mary is inseparably linked with the Christ-event* in the incarnation of the Logos by giving to it not only a human shape but a full hypostasis uniting in itself the two natures in full reciprocity and interpenetration. Early Greek patristic thought rejected the term *'Christotókos'* because it affected not the person of Mary, but the authentic, full understanding of the incarnation, i.e., the union without change and confusion of the two natures in Christ, right from the beginning.

The union of the two natures in the incarnation implies that Mary is *giving birth to God in time*. The whole of the Divine Logos came into full union with the whole of humanity by the birth of Christ. While the priority of this mystery belongs to the overwhelming power of God, Mary becomes the Mother of God by making this mystery possible, realising the paradoxical and extravagant and once for all event, that 'God appeared in the flesh' (1 Tim. 3:16) securing thus the equal sharing of two natures in one person.

That is why against the sectarian Christology, which results from the separation of the two natures by accepting only the human birth of Christ by Mary, the fathers opposed the right interpenetration of the two natures maintaining that 'since God is brought forth by Mary she is *Theotókos, giving birth to God and man at the same time'*.[1]

The insistence of early Christian theology on using only the term *'Theotókos'* is important and is a result of the appropriate understanding of Christology, i.e., in terms of the union in one person of the two natures, divine and human. Either one affirms by faith that this mystery occurred fully right from the beginning or one risks all kinds of deviation: dyophysitism (separating the two natures), monophysitism (accepting only one in the birth of Christ) or docetism (endorsing the idea of an 'appearance-like', but not the happening of the event itself). Behind this insistence there is the firm and self-evident conviction of faith in regard to the incarnation of the Logos that one cannot speak of nature (*physis*) outside a concrete person (*hypostasis*) without falling into an abstraction or negation of one of the two (in *Christotókos* the divine nature) and thereby destroying the full understanding of the incarnation. The *Theotókos stands within the right Christology as the proof and the guardian of the reality and fullness of the divine-human hypostatic union* in the form of a man conceived within humanity on the basis of full reciprocity, co-belongingness and union right from the beginning.

The Third Ecumenical Council of Ephesus (431) used a Christological term that pre-existed in the Eastern patristic tradition,[2] and so placed Mariology within Christology for ever. In the right Christology we affirm what happens in the incarnation of Logos, i.e., that 'He who was from the beginning as the eternal Logos, and Son of God took flesh from the Virgin *Theotókos* Maria and became fully man also'[3] and therefore 'if one does not accept and recognise the Holy Maria as *Theotókos* one is without a sense of divinity (in the incarnation).[4]

The *motherhood of Mary of the Logos* is not simply instrumental by giving flesh to the human appearance of the Logos. God does not take flesh for becoming a man; but he is doing so as the Divine Logos in full union and communion with the human nature *in one hypostasis* as it is operated by God, the Spirit, in Mary, i.e., the *Theotókos*. If this union is not seen in the birth of Christ out of the *synapheia* (association) of the two natures in Mary, then one doubles the persons (divine-human) in separation, confusing nature and person without distinction, maintaining neither divinity nor humanity in unison in one person. Maria, as the *Theotókos*, is the clear realisation, in a personal distinct way from the human side, of the mystery of the incarnation in full reciprocity and interpenetration of the two natures in one hypostasis-person without separation, fusion, change or confusion.

If human nature cannot be conceived and exist outside an hypostasis-person, it becomes evident that the Logos had to be born in human nature, fully, but containing together and inseparably the divine nature of the Logos, and the person giving him his human nature should operate it fully as a human person, i.e., becoming the *Theotókos* by this birth. Some Orthodox theologians go so far in their Christological interpretation of the *Theotókos* as to defend also the thesis that 'the *incarnation* is not only the union of the two natures in one hypostasis, but it *is also the union of the two hypostases in one nature*, because Christ has not brought his human nature from heaven and has not created it anew from the earth but he took it from the flesh and the blood of the very pure Virgin Maria'.[5]

(b) Mariology with Pneumatology

It is equally important not to conceive of Mariology independently of the operation of the Holy Spirit, but following the Christological approach implied in the *incarnation*. This is because the birth of Christ does not just occur between the Logos and Mary, but it is *operated by the Spirit*, as is recorded in the Bible (Luke 1:31ff.; Matthew 1:18-25) and confessed by the Creed ('born from the Holy Spirit and Maria the Virgin'). In this way we admit that the full divinity shares in the event of the incarnation of the Logos, who is born by the Father in eternity and sent to become the 'Son of Man' in the form of a slave. At the same time, the third divine hypostasis realises it in time since it, too, is sent by the Father.

With Mariology, in other words, we grasp the full deity in personal communion acting, creating, restoring and fulfilling the whole creation by operating in the humanity the saving act for all men in and through Mary. The Spirit's operation after the *annunciation* enacts the incarnation by his energy, in the same way as the resurrection of Christ does too, i.e., it is a matter of the mysterious entrance of God into and the departure from history, as at all of the key moments of Christ's life in time. By doing so, the Spirit does not allow the Logos-incarnation and presence to be limited to an I-Thou relationship with Maria, but, on the one hand, makes the whole Divinity share in the incarnation and, on the other hand, extends the impact of the divine economy to all people of the earth and at all times. The annunciation prefigures Pentecost and links the whole creation of God the Father from the beginning, elevating it by his operation in the Spirit, in virtue of the incarnate Logos. *Maria, as the* Theotókos, *is the personified humanity in full communion with the triune God*.

Without continuous reference to the operation of the Holy Spirit, the word about Maria loses its main focus as referring to the personal and also communal and cosmic dimension of the mystery of the incarnation. Mary is sharing in the mystery individually, as *Theotókos*, due to her extreme *obedience and humbleness* in the face of the will of God as expressed by the Spirit. She is the 'servant' of God, the poor and humble creature, but she operates the impossible in the eyes of men and becomes the fulfilment of the Old Testament prophecy and the unique elect person in history due to the operation of the Holy Spirit ('because the power of the Highest shall overshadow thee' (Luke 1:35)). She becomes pneumatophore, *Spirit-bearing*, in a special way, before she becomes Christophore or better *Theotókos*, Christ-bearing, so that in the incarnation the human contribution is enabled and fulfilled by God's special action in the Spirit on behalf of the whole of humankind.

Mariology with Pneumatology points to the fact that Mary never performs the paramount event of the birth of Christ alone; but God, in his full communion and personal relationship with humanity, is with her, enabling her to give the Logos human being and form. The Spirit, by his operation, personifies, realises *in time* and universalises the presence of the eternal Logos in time through a concrete human person at a specific moment in time, also. The annunciation reveals the personal link between God and humanity in Mary and thereafter personifies and renders the grace done in Christ ecclesial, universal, cosmic and perpetual in time. The Spirit renders the motherhood of *Theotókos* into the motherhood of the Ecclesia for all human beings.

The Logos-Maria relationship becomes God-humankind communion in the Ecclesia.

(c) Mariology for Ecclesiology

It becomes clear, therefore, that all Mariological remarks have a direct bearing on a deeper understanding of the Church as the Body of Christ, the communion of saints and the chosen people of God. Mary stands for our capacity to understand and have an access to the regathering of the whole of humankind into one pan-human family by a specific operation of the Holy Spirit. The personal election is fulfilled by the communal event. Between *annunciation and Pentecost* there is an inseparable organic link.

That is why the *Theotókos is regarded as the fufilment of the Old Testament prophecy and as the mother of the new people of God in the new covenant.* She is the typological figure of the 'daughter of Zion' (Isa. 62:11-12): 'Say ye to the daughter of Zion. Behold, thy salvation cometh . . . and they shall call them the Holy people, the redeemed of the Lord'; and Zephaniah 3:14ff.: 'Sing daughter of Zion; shout O Israel. . . . The Lord thy God in the midst of thee is mighty. . . . I will gather them that are sorrowful for the solemn assembly'.

Israel is always identified with a woman expecting salvation in humility and obedience in the new covenant. A direct link between the expectation of the *'daughter of Zion'* and the Ecclesia gathered through the fulfilment of the promise of God in her is recorded in Old and New Testament texts. There is a direct correspondence between Jeremiah's Lamentations (2:1-13) and St Luke's Benedictus (1:68-72) as well as the Magnificat (Luke 1:47-56). The 'daughter of Zion' as 'the Virgin' expects her salvation (Jer. Lam. 2:13) and is 'in pain and labours to bring forth' (Mich. 4:10); 'for as a young man marrieth a virgin, so shall thy sons marry thee; and as the bridegroom rejoiceth over the bride, so shall thy God rejoice over thee' (Isa. 62:5).

A typological exegesis of the many Old Testament texts figuring the 'daughter of Zion' led the early Church Fathers both in the East and the West to regard *Mary as the 'typos' of the Ecclesia* following the example of St Ambrosius: *'virgo quia est ecclesiae typus'*[6] and at the same time 'The Mother of all the living'.[7] It is the function of the Church as the mother in faith of the members of the Body of Christ that makes manifest the centrality of Mary as the *Theotókos* for ecclesiology. She is the first in this membership as the 'Mother of God' and becomes the Mother of the many in virtue of her basic role in the incarnation of the Logos. She is at the same time the *archetype of the final fulfilment* as the personification of the saved people of God at the end of times representing the event of the last days: God being with his people as it has been prefigured by the 'Emmanuel', God with us, by the operation of the Spirit in Mary.[8]

The *Theotókos*, in this sense, is sanctified by the Spirit and *prefigures as typos the holiness of the Church.* She shares in original sin but she is purified by the Spirit, in the same way that the Church is holy though she is composed of sinners. Clement of Alexandria finds in Mary the personification of the holiness of the Church ('Mary, the ever Virgin, the Holy Ecclesia').[9] As the fulfilment of the Old Testament prophecy, as mother of the new people of God, central personal focus of the then regathering and personification of the sanctification by the Spirit in expectation of the final triumph of grace, Mary shares in all the crucial stages of the divine economy recorded in the biblical text, as John Damascene remarks: 'the whole of the mystery of economy is operated in her'.[10]

As the *typos* of the Church and mother of all her members she appears in all the biblical narratives of the life of Christ and on the day of the foundation of the Church by the Spirit. One of the most significant events is the crucial moment of redemption, i.e., the Crucifixion. She is under the cross witnessing and giving thanks for salvation. Before Christ pronounces his final word 'All things now are accomplished' (John 19:28) he addresses first his mother pointing to John, the beloved disciple: 'Woman, behold thy Son' and then John: 'Behold thy mother' (19:27). Amongst all other possible ways of exegesis one has the right to interpret it typologically and in accordance with Eastern Orthodox hymnography and iconography and to see the organic link between the motherhood of God and the apostolic Church.[11] On this view the Church represents the central place of Mary from the human point of view as the *Theotókos*, within the whole story of redemption and her important role in the regathering of the people of God in virtue of Christ's sacrifice and the establishment in time of the communion of the Church in the Spirit.

2. DIVINE MOTHERHOOD BY GRACE AND FOR SANCTIFICATION AND DEIFICATION

The biblical reference to the person of Mary is centred around the operation of the Spirit. Everything that she is or performs is an *enactment of the grace of God operated in her*. She has not lived and acted by herself or for herself, but out of the grace of God and for the people of God. John Damascene, addressing her, underlines this fact: 'You have lived not for yourself but in God for whom you have come into life so that you serve the mystery of the salvation of all and God's will may be fulfilled through the incarnation of the Logos and the deification of us all'.[12] But this does not happen simply by an automatic operation of God's grace in her, as passively as through a lifeless vessel. The same Church father exalts her in these terms: 'You have received the full grace because you were fully worthy of it'.[13] She thus becomes a means, a symbol and a *typos* of the deification of all faithful who share by faith in the same mystery of the incarnation, cross and resurrection, through their co-operation with the same grace, based on their free will, in the image of the *Panhagia-Theotókos*.

(a) Sterility and Virginity

The decisive role of the grace of God is underlined in the Bible by the totally incomprehensible event of the incarnation thanks to the mysterious intervention of God. The main power of the weak, humble and poor Mary is that she is 'full of grace' according to the words of Gabriel (Luke 1:28). As unique, as fully *kecharitomene*, amongst all human beings, she gives birth to the divine Logos only by the intervention of God to the exclusion of the act of a man. The virgin birth becomes the self-evident mystery of faith, because it signifies the operation of overwhelming divine grace alone in the incarnation out of the humble but conscious and free consent of the virgin Mary: 'Behold the handmaid of the Lord; be it unto me according to thy word' (Luke 1:38).

To this divine intervention, which transcends natural laws, corresponds as an image of God's overwhelming power the birth of St John the Baptist out of an old and sterile woman, Elizabeth, to whom the angel of annunciations points at the same time (Luke 1:36). The virginity of Mary is prefigured by the birth out of sterility. The fulfilment of the Old Testament prophecy is the most mysterious event within the Old Testament prophecy. The last prophet becomes 'forerunner' of the prophesied Messiah. *The sterility becomes 'fruitful' and the virginity becomes motherhood par excellence in and through God's grace alone.* He who had created the first man out of his hands and his sovereign will alone on the basis of his being as love, he recreates now as Triune, and communion of love, the new man by a new sovereign act without the intervention of a man. Elizabeth and Mary stand for grateful humankind enabled to become a new beginning of authentic personal life from, in and for God alone reaffirming its total dependence on him. The sterility is thus fulfilled in the virginity. The impossibility of birth according to natural laws bcomes a full reality towards a new life. The visit of Mary to Elisabeth and their dialogue (Luke 1:39-56) contains the whole mystery of the divine economy and the relationship between the old and the new covenant. Their meeting points to the grace of God acting in both in a mysterious, but for faith in the most consistent and evident way.

The virgin birth is the key moment within the incarnation of the Logos. Without it the whole event is perverted as a human-centred natural happening. Orthodox patristics and hymnography have seen and praised this paradox as the norm and consistent act of God revealing himself, as Triune, in time, beyond human rationalisation and intervention. It kills the defiant form of men's virility as self-sufficiency and false self-creativity of life and points to the God-centred *creation ex-nihilo*, i.e., out of the fullness of his love, and it does so on the basis of the total free commitment and self-surrendering conscious obedience of the female, that is to say the receptive element of humanity. Mary, as the *new Eve*, becomes through grace the means for the restoration of humankind in its normal relationship in and with God. As sin has entered into history, now, in the same way communion is re-established through the grace of God alone but with the conscious obedience of a woman.

(b) Sinfulness and Holiness

Only on this basis (of the virgin birth) can we approach the next expression of the *paradox* of the biblical evidences of the incarnation. I mean the contradiction between the *fact of original sin inherited by the Theotókos* and the *birth of the Logos without sin*. And yet this is where the deepest mystery of the sanctification by the Spirit lies for Orthodox patristics. Sinful nature becomes pure and sinless existence. The immaculate conception can only be praised, but it cannot be made the subject of dogma. The sinfulness becomes inactive, while original sin remains with Mary as a human being. As a repentant sinner she is cleansed to become the mother of God though she remains in solidarity with the human race in the face of God, prefiguring the fact that the Logos of God will carry the sin of the world, because 'God hath made him to be sin' (2 Cor. 5:21) without, however, becoming a sinner.

Identity with sinful humanity is guaranteed but the sinless vocation into the new and grateful human reality is also affirmed and put into practice thereafter. The Eastern Orthodox praise the *Theotókos* as an immaculate (*aspilos*) virgin and mother but without making a dogma of her exemption from original sin. The understanding of the mystery of sanctification of the whole of sinful humankind as a dialectical process of repentant and sanctified sinner is contained in this paradox. Mary personifies in a unique way and becomes the *archetype of all human persons as sinners and restored at the same time by and in the ecclesial communion of saints.* The 'immaculate conception' taken literally is another rationalisation of the mystery from the human point of view, introducing as it does a gap between Mary and humankind in the most crucial and delicate issue of salvation. What one has to do is to maintain carefully the dialectical relationship between original sin and the sanctifying grace of God.[14]

(c) The Creation of the 'New Man'

The insistence of the Greek fathers on the solidarity of Mary with the Logos, on the one hand, and with full humanity permeated by the original sin, on the other, can be explained in terms of the Christological basis of their Mariology and the corresponding anthropology. The bestowal of divine motherhood through the grace of God is the basis for affirming the sonship of all human beings in the Spirit. Through the purification of her humanity she not only is the archetype of holiness but she becomes the mother of all of us who share in the incarnate Logos by the Spirit. The faithful incarnate the Logos spiritually and are fed by his blood and body. Mary is organically *linked with the eucharistic event* and its effects on the personal life of all believers.

It is the *Holy Spirit* who *forms Christ in the spirit of all men on the basis of Mary's sharing in the event of the incarnation.* The *Panhagia*, full of grace, reminds us in this respect of the words of Isaiah 54:1 for whom it is the sterile or desolate woman without husband becoming the mother of many who is praised. 'Full of grace' and 'sanctification' are in the image of the ·*Theotókos* identical.

The *Theotókos*, as the new Eve, has a part in striking to death the old enmity of man by bringing forth the Logos, who 'makes in himself of twain one new man so making peace' (Eph. 2:15) so that all men can from now on (by free will, in the image of the *Theotókos*, who is the first and unique in the midst of them and in full solidarity with them) 'put on the new man, which after God is created in righteousness and true holiness' (Eph. 4:24).

It is on this basis that one has to understand Christ's words of answer to those who informed him that his mother and his brothers wanted to speak to him: 'Behold my mother and my brethren. . . . These who shall do the will of my Father which is in heaven' (Matt. 12:49-50): he pointed to the extended motherhood and brotherhood. It reminds us also of his words: 'He that loveth father or mother more than me is not worthy of me' (Matt. 10:35). It is the spiritual parenthood that is far beyond the natural one, which is meant here. It is in this sense that Christ addresses Mary as 'Woman' instead of as mother, for he points to the new situation of motherhood being extended to the communion of the elect people of God. That is where *Mary's motherhood has passed so as to become a new reality creating the 'new man' in Christ.* The will of God has always been and is revealed and enacted in Mary: 'the incarnation of the Logos and of our own deification'.[15]

It is the Ecclesia which, from the human point of view, bears in her midst the *Theotókos* that continues to give birth as mother of us all through the sanctification of the Holy Spirit. The motherhood of Mary is realised within the new covenant as a perpetual spiritual rebirth of the many. Mary, as *Theotókos*, has not simply given flesh to the Logos. She has not given human shape to Jesus of Nazareth alone. She gave the hyman hypostatis to the Logos as the new Adam and shared in the reconciliation between God and man.[16]

3. THE *THEOTÓKOS* AND THE NEW HUMAN PERSON IN A NEW WORLD

The solidarity of the *Theotókos* with the human condition in the deepest weakness and powerlessness of man has to become a shaking of the foundations of all of our self-centred power structures and conceptions of the Church, and of our social life as well as of the anthropocentric humanisms thought up in the ivory towers of our vanity seeking power and domination over others. The Mother of God is *as 'typos' the servant of the Lord*; she shared in his sufferings and bore witness to his glory in silence and humility. The honour addressed to her by the Church in worship is due to her role in the incarnation. She is conscious that hers is a reflected glory, and her sharing in this is because God had appreciated the 'low estate of his hand-maiden'; this is why 'from henceforth all generations shall call me blessed' (Luke 1:48).

Mary in the Eastern Orthodox tradition is honoured and glorified for her humility in all manner of majestic hymns and prayers. It is a glorious treasure in world literature and makes a perpetual doxology and thanksgiving of the whole of orthodox worship. The Athakist Hymn during the period of Lent, the fifteen days of intercessions early in August, the central focus of Mary in every gathering of the Church for worship make Orthodox worship a paramount veneration of the *Theotókos* as she personifies the fact that all the faithful are a receptacle of grace in the process of repentance and regeneration. But what are praised in all of these glorious acts of worship are the suffering weakness, and the humble obedience.

That is why, though in its hymns the Eastern Tradition seems to adopt the idea of the 'bodily assumption' of the *Theotókos*, because one cannot admit that the body which held the divine Logos could ever perish,[17] the teaching of the Church confessed unanimously that the *Theotókos* fully shared in the death of all human beings. It thus excluded another separation of the *Theotókos* from the misery of the human condition as in the case of the immaculate conception. The greatest celebration of the Virgin Mary is therefore called in the Church calendar (15th of August) the feast of the 'Dormition of the *Theotókos*' and it is meant to bring out the relevance of her hidden glory as the obedient servant of the Lord for the spirituality and vision of life of all celebrants.

(a) Power in weakness

The dominant characteristic of the Virgin Mary as the 'typos' of the holiness of the Church is, for the Eastern tradition, that of a *powerless person redeemed and so become a grateful sinner thanks to her total obedience and utmost humility* in the face of God. She is the personification of the words of St Paul that God 'has chosen the weak things of the world to confound the things which are mighty' (I Cor. 1:27). She followed and realised in her life the sense of the 'kenosis' of the Logos, to whom she gave the human hypostasis, as he made himself of no reputation and took upon him the 'form of a servant' (Phil. 2:7).

The conscious acceptance of human weakness as the main element of the new human person in Christ is the chief characteristic of the Christian anthropology based on the 'typos' of the Mother of God as *Theotókos*. The fact is, however, that in this weakness the glory of the Almighty is manifested as a paradox and folly for human reason, shaking the foundations of the self-sufficiency of man, the structures of the human mind and society and causing the most radical changes in hierarchical institutions, in unjust orders of human enterprises and making the powerful of the world miserable human beings and rich men 'empty'.

One of the most earth-shaking texts in the Bible is the one that refers in this sense to the exaltation of Mary on account of her weakness: the well-known Magnificat of the *Theotókos* (Luke 1:49-53). God has 'done to me great things', and these words are followed by an analysis at three successive levels of these 'great things done to her', which make manifest the triumph of weakness against illegitimate man-centred pride, mighty leaders and rich people. In the figure of the *Theotókos*, these threefold power-structures of humanity (pride, exousia-authority and material wealth), are challenged and their permanence is shaken and finally destroyed. This text, summarising the best of the Old Testament prophecy, is put by the gospel in the mouth of the thanksgiving Virgin Mary as its culminating figure and as the means by which the new human person in Christ is to be present dynamically in all human conditions so as to bring about radical changes in personal ethics and social structures of injustice. The weakness of Mary realises the power of God in concrete human reality, becoming in this way the eternal *typos of the basic truth in Christian anthropology*.

Unfortunately, seeking power in wisdom and authority as they do, even within Church structures and theology, Christians of all traditions are inclined to turn this text into a glorious hymn in an emotional way and to empty it of its dynamic impact on their life and its revolutionary mission against themselves and against all kinds of injustice caused by the illegitimate use of power in the world. The *Theotókos*, being the incarnation of the power of God in human weakness, has been thus alienated from her most important role in a Church community struggling in the world and risks not making the appropriate impact on Christians in the shape of conceiving and realising the 'new man' as the new human person in Christ. Further, the Eastern Orthodox tradition, due to its exaggerated emphasis on praise, *risks remaining passive* in the face of this dynamic archetype of a consistent revolutionary action in all realms of personal and collective life permeated by the vanity of human pride and the illegitimate thirst for power. Ceremonial glory and human sentimentality threaten to negate the right and self-evident effects of the dynamic prototype of the *Theotókos* in personal and social ethics.

Fortunately, historical conditions have exposed most of the ancient Orthodox churches to harsh martyrdom and so have revealed the dialectics of weakness to them. The *Theotókos* thus became their central focus and consolation. She preserved them in their very weakness as the people of God, regardless of their structures and external appearance, creating as their backbone a series of weak and desolate figures, the martyrs, as living witnesses of the example of the servant suffering in the image of the *Panhagia*. It remains to be seen how in some line of witness she can inspire a dynamic Orthodox attitude in the secular context of social injustice.

(b) Female and Male Person in salvation

It is impossible to refer to the *Theotókos* Maria without appreciating the restoration of the relationship between the two sexes through the incarnation of the Logos appearing in human form as a man but containing both sexes without discrimination or qualitative priority of the one over the other, and effected by a woman without the interference of a man. The *parthenogenesis* (the virgin birth) contributes in a special way to this restoration by reversing the order of the fall in the biblical narrative of the entrance of original sin into the human race. Now, the *new Eve enjoys priority in grace* for all men over against the one who allowed temptation to enter into the whole of humankind.

The *Theotókos*, seen from this angle and in this prospective, stands as a woman for the whole of humanity elevated together as male and female, and restored and called upon to become together 'new Persons in Christ'. Just as the original temptation involved both female and male through a woman so now by the incarnation through the *Theotókos* the whole of the human race is restored by a woman. It was not so much that temptation was effected through the 'weak' sex of humanity but that the whole of humanity in solidarity of sin had been tempted in the woman as representing the receptive element of grace and life, and at the same time freedom was abused resulting in the breaking of communion with God (which is the essence of sin) so that the order of creation and creativity whose 'typos' is the male element was shaken. The female person's sharing alone in the act of salvation by the incarnate Logos appearing in the form of a male person, a man in history, recapitulates the whole of humanity in solidarity receiving grace, denoting par excellence the receptive element of life in God's act of creation. *The elevation of the* Theotókos *is the elevation of the whole of humankind as male and female persons in absolute union and deep qualitative equality by God's creative and saving act.*

Within this solidarity and equality the *Theotókos* points to the specific *God-given role of the female person as the receptive element in salvation* underlining the grace from God alone. This role incarnates the benevolent tenderness in God's creation out of love, as his essence. By electing the virgin Maria to incarnate the Logos, God has elected what is tender, loving and personifying in His creation and rejected what is harsh and attacking, the virile-masculine-male power-centred role that penetrates by violence. Paul Evdokimov, who represents this interpretation of the *Theotókos*, analyses rightly the two roles female-male in the saving act of God, praising the female one as that which represents the receiving-offering-sacrificing element in the form of 'the lamb of God immolated before the foundation of the world'. God refuses the 'masculine solution as violent extroverted creativity in the service of man's power and domination', since for man after the fall to live signifies to possess, to conquer, to struggle to the end and kill, while for woman (after the incarnation in the person of Mary) to live is 'to give birth, to preserve and protect live by giving herself; a man gives himself in order to win a victory, while a woman saves by becoming herself an offering'.[18] In this destiny, the female person, in the person of Mary, realises the eternal God-given place and role of the whole of humanity restored back by the incarnate Logos to the normal communal relationship of love and freedom with its Creator.

(c) *Theotókos*: the eschatological vision of the new human person

One of the most dynamic and majestic images of the Bible is the one in the Book of Revelation of 'a great portent in heaven, a woman clothed with the sun . . . with the moon under her feet and on her head a crown of twelve stars; she was with child and she cried out in her pangs of birth, in anguish of delivery' against whom and her child the 'red dragon' is fighting without success as the woman is covered by the grace of God and preserved 'with her child in the desert' to be fed and protected there by God (Rev. 12:1-17).

This image summarises in the most vivid colours the process of the eternal regeneration of life after the incarnation and the struggle for the creation of the 'new man' as the new human person in Christ towards its final fulfilment through the grace of God at the end of times. Almost all of the Church Fathers in the East and the West, as well as the Reformers and modern exegetes who interpreted this text, have seen in this image the Church, on the basis of the birth of Christ 'by a woman' as the mother of restored humanity in Christ.[19] This image in the closing chapters of the Bible summarises the divine economy in view of the perpetual struggle 'in travail' towards the spiritual rebirth of all of the faithful. They have to conform themselves to the example of a hard life of suffering against sin but they are in glory in the light of the final victory over evil by the divine motherhood of the *Theotókos* in the Church. She is the central figure, the *archetype given by God to humanity struggling towards the creation of the new human person in Christ and in his Church.*[20]

EPILOGUE

It is clear what great importance the word about Mary has for Church life, theology and especially for Christian anthropology today. It becomes imperative to speak today of a Mariological anthropology if we are to deal Christologically with the place of the virgin Mary in the economy of salvation and of her motherhood in the Church.[21] In particular, it can help us to open another horizon in our discussion of the burning issue of man and woman's community in Church and society. The elevation and exaltation of Mary as *Theotókos* and *Panhagia* can illustrate a new approach to the *priority of the female element*. In a distinct and special way the female stands over the male in the process of salvation and formation of the new human person in repentance, humility, poverty, social justice and change of unjust structures in their patriarchical, one-sided virile-masculine inflexibility devoid of charismatic essence and function in today's technocratic world and mechanised social life.

On the other hand, it can teach us the guide-lines of an *evangelical feminism, which is not based on equal rights through equal functions of man and woman*. This attitude deprives humanity of that fundamental differentiation in which consists its beauty, goodness and joy. The 'virilisation' of woman for the sake of fighting against sexism sets the solution of the problem on the wrong track if it is judged by the function of Mary in the history of salvation. The female element in Christian faith is the dominant one in terms of communal essence of humanity taken as a whole, and to it the male has to be conformed by negating its thirst for power and domination. It is not the female, therefore, that has to identify itself with the male in order to secure equality. In the light of an authentic Mariology, such an attitude violates humanity by abandoning it to its hard onesided virile function through a false and perverted use of power.

Consequently, the *Theotókos* can also *influence all the structures* of the Church, rendering its ministry more charismatic and flexible, taking away its despotism, clericalism and false ministerial functionalism. In so far as hierarchical orders are reserved to men, they are continuously challenged to realise their witness of service in love in the image of the 'typos' of the Church as it is represented by the *Panhagia* in the midst of the people of God.

That is why the *Theotókos* has also a direct *bearing on ecumenical work*. Her motherhood in the Church is a direct appeal for the unity of the Church on a charismatic basis by way of inviting our mutual repentance in the face of God and in obedience to him. We have to grow into 'the mature stature of a man' in faith (Eph. 4:13) by appreciating the charismata of the 'woman ' as *Theotókos*, who as the Mother unites all members of the Body of Christ in one undivided family in unbroken continuity. Church representatives within the ecumenical movement today realise more and more the need to refer to Mary as the focus of unity from the human side. All kinds of extremist positions about the place of the *Theotókos* in efforts towards unity and in ecclesiology, are slowly but progressively undergoing a change of attitudes.

In the eyes of an Eastern Orthodox believer the return of Roman Catholicism during and after the Second Vatican Council to a genuine Christological Mariology that avoids dogmatic exaggerations and reaffirms her solidarity with the Christian community,[22] is very encouraging, as is also the renewed interest that Reformed theology has in ecumenical circles to return to teaching of the great Reformers about the important ecclesiological significance of the virgin Mary for today, by stating: ' . . . the idea of Mary as a symbol of the Church could, nevertheless, still be of value, particularly for the churches of Reformation. It could remind them of a dimension they have largely lost. As symbol of the Church, Mary reminds us that the community of faith is not simply a community in the present moment only but one which continues through the centuries'.[23]

Eastern Orthodox are expected to contribute to these converging lines in Mariology with a fresh dynamic interpretation and, beyond all kinds of ceremonialism, of the central place of the *Theotókos* in the ecclesial community. Apart from the very rich and justified veneration of the *Theotókos* by their worshipping community, they have to make a careful study of the relevance to today's ecclesiological debate in ecumenical circles and especially to actual problems in Church and social life in order to be able to share, along with other Christian traditions, in the effort to build a just community of women and men in and through the Ecclesia.

Notes

1. 'St. John Damascene: Ekthesis of Orthodox Faith' in D. Nellas *The Theotókos* (in Greek) III, 2 (Athens 1970) p. 24.

2. Alexandros of Alexandria (+ 328) first used this term Christologically: *Nicolas Cavasilas: The Theometor* D. Nellas (Athens 1968) p. 24.

3. Athanasios the Great, Migne P. G. 26, 385 quoted by J. Kalogirou in: *Maria the Ever-Virgin*

Theotókos *according to the Orthodox Faith* (Salonica 1957) p. 36. The term in this sense is to be found in Athanasios in several places: see P. G. 26, 349-393-517 etc.

4. Gregory of Nazianzan, Migne P. G. 37, 177 quoted by J. Kalogirou, in the work cited in note 3, at p. 37.

5. Serge Boulgakov *Du Verbe Incarné*, (Translated from Russian by C. Andronikoff), (Paris 1982) p. 128.

6. Migne P. L. 15, 1555 quoted by P. Nellas in the work cited in note 1, at p. 25.

7. Epiphanios of Cyprus, Migne P. G. 42,728.

8. See more on this point in *L'Orthodoxie* by P. Evdokimov in the chapter 'L'aspect mariologique de l'Eglise' pp. 148-154 (Paris 1959).

9. P. G. 77, 996 quoted by P. Evdokimov in the work cited in note 8, at p. 149.

10. Quoted by P. Nellas in the work cited in note 1, at p. 26.

11. On the different possible interpretations of this text see Max Thurian: *Marie Mère du Seigneur; Figure de l'Eglise* (Les Presses de Taizé 1962) at pp. 212-231. Also concerning the Old Testament basis for understanding the role of Mary in the mystery of the covenant, see the chapter 'The Daughter of Zion', *ibid.* p. 19 ff.

12. *On the Orthodox Faith* A9, quoted by P. Nellas, in the work cited in note 1, at p. 25.

13. *Ibid.* B8 p. 27.

14. On the attitude of the Eastern Orthodox see John Kalogirou: *Mary the ever virgin* Theotókos *according to the Orthodox Faith* (Salonica 1957) pp. 10-30 (in Greek) and the articles of Prof. H. Alivisatos and P. Bratsiotis mentioned in the bibliography.

15. St John Damascene *On Orthodox Faith* B1, quoted by P. Nellas in the work cited in note 1, at p. 26.

16. On this point see the excellent chapters of Max Thurian: *Marie et l'Eglise* p. 175-253.

17. This idea is clearly expressed by M. Siotis in *The appearance of the church service to the Theotókos and the church tradition regarding her Dormition* (Salonica 1950) p. 16 (in Greek).

18. The exact words of P. Evdokimov in the original French text are: 'il refuse la solution masculine au gloire, comme il rejètte les solutions masculines des trois tentations au désert et choisit l'offrande de soi, son oblation, la figure de l'agneau immolé. Pour l'homme, vivre c'est conquérir, lutter, tuer; pour la femme, c'est enfanter, entretenir, protéger la vie en se donnant. L'homme se donne pour remporter la victoire, la femme sauve en devenant pure offrande' (Paul Evdokimov: *La Femme et le Salut du Monde*, Paris 1958 p. 151).

19. Again see for the interpretation of this text and especially its link with the Old Testament prophecy Max Thurian in the work cited in note 16, pp. 262 to 281.

20. It is again Paul Evdokimov who develops the impact of this eschatological image for Christian anthropology. He refers also to the well known psychoanalytical interpretation of chapter 12 of the Book of Revelation by C. G. Jung in his book *Antwort auf Hiob* in this context and takes a positive stance to it from an Eastern Orthodox point of view (see P. Evdokimov in the work cited in note 18 at p. 196. See especially for our subject Chapter III. 'La Theotókos, Archétype du Féminin' p. 207-221.

21. Wolfgang Beinert, dealing with the relevance of Mariology today, concludes with the same emphasis from another angle by writing: 'The great themes of the study on Mary do not remain in isolation from each other, but they are guide lines of unity in theological anthropology'. In *Heute von Maria reden*? (Freiburg-Basel-Wien 1973) p. 108.

22. See the the work of Walter Delius *Geschichte der Marienverehrung* (Munich-Basel 1963) and of René Laurentin *Bilan du Concile* (Paris 1963) and his book *La Question Mariale* (Paris 1963) and also the Symposium edited by P. Stater Maria in *Der Offenbarung* (3. Paderborn 1962).

23. Lukas Vischer: 'Mary—Symbol of the Church and Symbol of Humankind' in *Mid-Stream* No. 1 (January 1978) p. 12.

See also the very interesting collection of articles on the ecumenical importance of Mariology published by the Ecumenical Society of the blessed Virgin Mary, International Ecumenical Conference (London and Oxford 1979) 'Looking Forward' in the review *One in Christ* (1980) No

1-2 pp. 54-154.

See also the ecumenical symposium *La Vierge Marie* (Paris 1968) pp. 1-166, R. Beaupère (Introduction) and the authors P. Zobel, M. Caplain, H. Roux, A. Kniazeff.

Bibliography (Orthodox)

Boulgakof, S. *Du verbe Incarné* (Traduit du Russe par C. Andronikof) (Paris 1982) (especially pp. 103-137.

Brock, S. 'Mary and the Eucharist' in *Sobornost* no. 2 (1979) pp. 50-60.

Clément, O. 'Féminisme Russe et Mère de Dieu' 'Chronique: Réponse à l'enquête du Conseil Oecuménique des Eglises in *Contacts* XXXe Année (3e Trimestre 1980) pp. 361-376.

Damascène, Jean *Homelies sur la Nativité et la Dormition* (Paris 1961) (Sources Chrétiènnes) (especially the introduction by P. Voulet S.J. pp. 8-40).

Evdokimov, P. *L'Orthodoxie* (Paris et Neuchatel 1959) (especially pp. 148-170 'L'aspect mariologique de l'Eglise').

Evdokimov, P. *La Femme et le salut du monde. Etude d'anthropologie chrétienne sur les charismes de la femme* (Tournai-Paris 1958).

Gillet, L. *Marie, Mère de Jésus* in *Contacts*, XXXe Année, No. 108 (1979) pp. 361-376.

Kniazeff, A. *Mariologie biblique et liturgie Byzantine* (1955/3) pp. 268-289.

Lossky, V. *Essai sur la théologie mystique de l'Eglise d'Orient* (Paris 1944).

Lossky, V. *In the Image and the Likeness of God* (New York 1974) especially ch. 11; *Panagia*, pp. 195-210.

Sherwood, P. 'Byzantine Mariology' in *Eastern Churches Quarterly* Vol. XIV No. 8 (Winter 1962) 384-410.

Thornton, L. S., Lossky, V., Mascall, E. L., Florovsky, G., Parker, T. M., Gillet, L. (an Anglican-Orthodox Symposium) *The Mother of God* (London 1949).

Bibliography (in Greek)

Dratselas, K. *The* Theotókos *and the Akathist Hymn* (Trikala and Athens) 1957.

Kalogirou, John *Maria, the ever Virgin* Theotókos *according to the Orthodox Faith* (Salonica) Reprint from the Review *Gregorios Palamas* (1957) pp. 1-176.

Kavasilas, Nikolaos *The Theometor*, ed. P. Nellas (Introduction and commentaries by P. Nellas) (Athens 1968) pp. 1-225.

Metelinaios, E. *The* Theotókos *Maria, the Daughter of the Prophets* (Apostoliki Diakonia Press 1961).

Theodorou, Andreas *The Daughter of the Kingdom. A Theological Commentary on the Akathist Hymn* (Athens 1977) pp. 1-278.

Trembelas, P. *The Mother of the Saviour* (Athens 1958).

Articles

Concerning the promulgation of the new dogmas on Mary by the Roman Catholic Church.

Alivisatos, H. 'The New Dogma' in *Ekklesia* (Athens 1950) 354ff. and 368ff.

Brátsiotis, P. 'On account of the new Dogma in *Ekklesia* (Athens 1950) 398ff.

Farantos, M. 'The Place and the Importance of the *Theotókos* in the Life and Faith of the Church' in *Dogmatic and Ethic Subjects* (Athens 1983) pp. 259-279.

Metropolitan Ireneus of Samos 'The new Dogma of the Roman Church' in *Ekklesia* (Athens 1950) p. 396ff.

Kalogirou, J. 'Maria' in *Religious and Ethics Encyclopedia* VIII (Athens 1966) pp. 649-685.

Kalokuris, K. 'Maria' (Iconography) *ibid.*, pp. 685-707.

Karmiris, J. 'The new Dogma of the Roman Church' in *Ekklesia* (Athens 1951) p. 21-25.

Papadopoulos, S. 'The ever Virgin Mary' in *Religious and Ethics Encyclopedia* I (Athens 1962) pp. 462-472.

Siotis, M. 'On the Worship of the Dormition of the *Theotókos*. The Church Tradition' in *Grigorios Palamas Review* (Salonica 1950) pp. 187-192.

Gottfried Maron

Mary in Protestant Theology

1. PRESUPPOSITIONS

IF WE are to understand the Reformation even in relation to the theme of Mariology, we must take into account the situation in the late middle ages. Here this situation is illustrated in a particularly significant manner. *Dogmatically* very little was clearly defined in the medieval Church, only the fundamental facts of the *virgin birth* (the Creed: '*natus ex Maria virgine*', 'born of the virgin Mary'), and of the title *Mother of God* (Ephesus 431: *Theotókos*, amplified, safeguarded and limited by Chalcedon 451: '*ex Maria Virgine . . . secondum humanitatem*', 'born of the Virgin Mary . . . according to the manhood') are not in dispute. There were, however, as yet no 'Marian dogmas'.

Theologically this means considerable freedom and variety. However, the axiom '*De Maria nunquam satis*' ('of Mary enough can never be said'), which was not without its dangers, was a stimulus to ingenious intellectual speculations. Above all, the question of Mary's collaboration in the work of salvation was discussed. From the thirteenth century there were theological excesses, for example, St Bernardino of Siena (1380-1444) cannot be acquitted of questionable theological aberration. Classical scholasticism dealt with the theme of Mary's freedom from original sin. A debate which lasted for centuries began between Dominicans and Franciscans, concerning the immaculate conception of Mary. However, the question under debate was never settled on its merits, the dispute on this theme being forbidden by Sixtus IV in 1482-1483. The final outcome of this was that the doctrine of the immaculate conception of Mary (developed principally by Duns Scotus) was protected against the violent attacks of Dominicans. At the same time the festival was approved, but not made obligatory on the Church.

Great freedom prevailed in the field of *practical devotion*. In Marian festivals Mary was given a significant place with hymns and prayers. Marian legends were handed down, images and holy shrines of Mary were honoured, Mary became a central theme of Christian art. It must, however, be noted that in the late middle ages, Marian piety, in spite of the sixteenth-century tendency to give it an independent place, still remained embedded in the wider context of the veneration of the saints. With regard to the late middle ages even a Catholic author can speak of a *nadir*, and say 'A purge was necessary' (R. Laurentin).

40

2. HISTORICAL RETROSPECT

(a) Martin Luther and the Reformation

(i) Even the utterances of Martin Luther (1483-1546) concerning Mary are to be seen in the context of his central theological and Christological doctrine, as it is summed up in his understanding of justification. Luther frequently describes his point of departure; it is the late medieval picture of the Last Judgment. In this Mary played the part of a mediator for poor sinners, even in contrast with her Son, for 'we held Christ to be our angry Judge, and Mary our mercy-seat, in whom alone was all our trust and refuge'. But this means for Luther to take away from Christ his office, and to give it to Mary (WA 30, II, 299: 1530). With the recognition of Christ as the gracious brother *pro nobis*, the significance of *Mary* as our most important helper in judgment and extremity disappears, she *loses* her immediate *soteriological function*, though indeed she continues to be an important figure in the story of salvation. This explains Luther's theological polemical interest in the theme as a reformer. Luther's theological understanding of Mary is strongly theocentric and Christocentric. In his eyes it finds reinforcement in a return to the dogmatic foundations of the ancient Church, and is replenished with biblical content. Above all, for him the virgin birth stands unshaken. In addition, the term *'Theotókos'* of the Council of Ephesus is reaffirmed without question. On the contested theological doctrine of the immaculate conception Luther does not express himself unambiguously.

On the other hand, *as an exegete*, Luther can say important things about Mary, above all in his interpretation of the Magnificat of 1521 (WA 7, 544-604). His aim is not to 'exalt' Mary; it is precisely her humility that is emphasised, in order to praise the greatness of the act of God's mercy. It was through grace that she became the mother of God, not through merit! In this sense one can indeed speak of a 'panegyric of Mary' in Luther: *'creatura Maria non potest satis laudari'* as a created being Mary cannot be enough praised' (WA TR 1, 219 no. 494). 'The poor maid' is a model of humility, etc., but we must not make her 'the queen of heaven', for that means to dishonour Christ, by ascribing to a creature what belongs to God alone (WA 10 III, 22: 1522).

For Luther and the Reformers Mary is not a significant theme of theological controversy. Luther's polemic is aimed essentially at the praxis, *the false honour done to Mary*. It is at the point in religious practice where Christ is dispossessed and his 'office' taken from him that in Luther's opinion this *'abusus'* (misuse) becomes evident, and for that reason he even wished to see 'the cult of Mary' 'eradicated' (WA 11, 61: 1522). With great frequency we find him repudiating the *'Salve Regina'*, where Mary is called *'regina misericordiae'* (queen of mercy) and *'vita, dulcedo et spes nostra'* (our life, sweetness and hope). The *'regina coeli'* is also repudiated.

Thus Luther's interest as a reformer consists in a purification of public worship and the Christian Year from the misuse of festivals and forms, i.e., in a Christological adjustment. Thus even Marian festivals are left in existence, the Annunciation to Mary, 25 March; the Visitation of Mary, 2 July; the Purification of Mary, 2 February), so far as they are based on Scripture. The Reformers indeed set store by underlining the relation of these festivals to Christ himself, indeed by celebrating them directly as *festivals of Christ*. And yet these days were used also to treat of Mary and her significance for Protestant Christians. Mary retained her place in these festivals.

(ii) Among the other Reformers *Huldrich Zwingli* (1484-1531), as a contemporary of Luther's, stands very near to him. On this point he is less polemical, and does not deny his stronger humanistic formation and spiritualising tendency. The ancient Christian dogma is accepted and defended. Mary is an *instrument* of salvation-history, and a *model* of Christian life, a *sign* and a *witness*, who points to the miracle and mystery of Christ. For Zwingli, too, teaching about Mary is a part of teaching about Christ: 'All her honour is her Son' (Z I, 426), she cannot allow 'that she should be given the honour that belongs to her Son' (Z II, 195). Zwingli also retains to the last the Marian festivals, but decisively opposes the religious veneration of Mary, and strictly forbids men to worship her, even to call upon her. True honour is done to Mary by caring for the poor.

(iii) Among the younger Reformers *Philip Melanchthon* (1497-1560) is less marked by medieval piety, and is more deeply stamped by humanistic traits. In essentials he follows Martin Luther, but his general bearing is more prosaic, and yet even he can speak warmly of Mary as '*dignissima aplissimis honoribus*' ('she is worthy of the very highest praise' (Apology for the Confession of Augsburg, XIII). Her immaculate conception, invented by the monks, was, of course 'a frivolous thing' (CR 25, 898). However Mary stands in the traditional line of the saints as a model, she is '*a type of the Church*': '*Maria semper representat Ecclesiam* ('Mary eternally represents the Church') (CR 14, 152).

(iv) John Calvin (1509-1564) clearly belongs to the second generation of the Reformers. In spite of his substantial adherence to the decrees of the ancient councils, he expresses his misgivings about the title 'mother of God'. Mary is ensnared in original Sin, Christ alone does not come under judgment. Among the Papists Mary has become an 'idol', for which reason Calvin vigorously rejects her invocation, and hope of her advocacy and intercession, as 'damnable blasphemy'; in Geneva all festivals of Mary, the Apostles and the saints were suppressed, for Christians owe to God alone worship and veneration. This does not hinder Calvin from praising the '*sancta virgo*' (holy virgin) as a teacher and model in faith, the praise of God and knowledge of the Scriptures.

(b) Protestant Orthodoxy, Pietism, and the Enlightenment

The Roman Catholic background must be kept in mind also in relation to the development in succeeding years, especially the fact that the official doctrinal documents of the Church exercise great reserve in relation to Mary (Tridentinum, Roman Cathechism). Also, it was not until the Counter-Reformation was under way that the veneration of the saints in fact concentrated itself upon Mary (K. Rahner). Further, it was not till the last decades of the sixteenth century that there came into being an independent theological Mariology (Canisius 1577, Suarez 1590). In praxis as well as in theory, Spain and the Jesuit Order took a leading place.

(i) *Protestant Orthodoxy*

Protestant orthodoxy is primarily interested in theological doctrine. Both in its positive exposition of dogma, and in its polemical contrast of doctrinal positions, it starts with the officially formulated texts on both sides. The result of this is that the Marian theme is only touched *incidentally*, and has no section devoted to it even in the great controversial writings of the time. For example Martin Chemnitz (*Examen Concilii Tridentini*, 1563-1573) or Johann Gerhard (*Confessio Catholica* 1634-1637) treat of Mary under different headings, especially in dealing with original sin and the veneration of the saints. Real knowledge of the later practical and theological developments on the Roman Catholic side is seldom found, as in Conrad Dannhauer, who recognises that the Jesuits are leaders in Marian spirituality, and fears that 'it all ends up in Mariosophy'.

In the exposition of their own doctrine their interest in the figure of Mary is less than that of the Reformers. Mary is given less and less place in the work of the Protestant dogmatic writers, inasmuch as a decline of interest is to be observed in the series of writers starting with Johann Gerhard, continuing with Quenstedt (1685), Hollatz (1707) and Buddeus (1723) and concluding with Baier (1750). There are few monographs on the subject.

(ii) *Pietism* is in many respects akin to Protestant orthodoxy; Philipp Jakob Spener

(1635-1705) is for example an outstanding controversial theologian. And although the Pietists have a more marked interest in the *praxis pietatis* (practice of religion), and a fuller knowledge of the life of the other confession, the theme of Mary is nowhere given special attention in the pietistic controversial writings (Paul Anton, 1732; Johann Jakob Rambach, 1738). Even in the conversations of Graf Zinzendorf (1750-1760) with Cardinal Noailles, the Archbishop of Paris, the theme is soteriology and ecclesiology, not questions of Mariology, although Zinzendorf has a sensitive understanding of the 'feminine' element in religion.

(iii) In the theological *Enlightenment* the theme recedes further. In Siegmund Jacob Baumgarten's *Geschichte der Religionspartheyen* (1766) Mary is given three pages out of 1,300. Johann Salomo Semler emphatically rejects every kind of veneration of Mary, and regards it as part of the superstition of the Roman Church. The ideal of the natural–the reasonable is dominant. The fading of the religious impulse is, however, counterbalanced by a growing interest in ethical and ethico-social questions. The situation on the Catholic side corresponds to this in many respects, thus revealing a pervasive trend in the intellectual history of Europe.

Even on the Catholic side the time 1750-1850 is a '*sterile epoch*' (Laurentin) in respect of Marian piety, a situation which at the same time indicates the vigorous and continuing influence of rationalistic thought until far into the nineteenth century. The consequences for the life of the Church are to be seen everywhere. In the second half of the eighteenth century in the Protestant churches the Marian festivals, which up to that time had been still celebrated as full holidays, were gradually discouraged, first decreed as half-holidays and then abolished. Admittedly, there was another side to the Enlightenment. In Johann Gottfried Herder, the source of so many innovations, we see already the reaction. A sermon by him on Mary, dating from the year 1773, has been preserved, whose content to a great extent agrees with Reformation teaching and lays emphasis on 'the Maid' in Luther's sense. But it was precisely in this that Mary was great 'and as such let us honour her'.

(c) From the Nineteenth Century to the Present

The breakthrough to a new understanding came not from the theologians, but in the realm of art and literature; in *Romanticism*, which was one of the greatest transformations in the intellectual climate of modern times. Novalis the poet expresses himself forcibly:

Mother, who thee once hath seen
Wholly lost hath never been.—

And many poets say the like. Certainly at this point the question arises with urgency: Is this a secularisation of biblical and Christian concepts? Are people really speaking about Mary, or about 'Woman', or 'the eternal feminine'? In Schleiermaher's *Weihnachtsfeier* (1806) it is significantly said that 'every mother can be called a Mary'.

This habit of honouring *Mary* as a *symbol of motherhood*, within the limits of a purely human religiosity, continued outside the Protestant Church. Feuerbach, the great critic of Christianity, could write in his *Wesen des Christentums* (1841) 'The father is only a reality where the mother is a reality' and take Protestantism to task for setting aside the Mother of God—an action which flew in the face of the anthropological facts, and would cost it dear. Even Paul de Lagarde, the bitter critic of 'Jewish' Paulinism, reproaches Protestantism with its exclusively male emphasis, and pleads the necessity of a Madonna cult in 'German religion'.

(i) *Protestant Reaction to the Dogma of the Immaculate Conception*

Within Protestant Christendom there was a revival of an interest in the figure of

Mary, partly in Pietism and partly in the church, in the *revival movement* and in Lutheran *Confessionalism*, here represented principally by Löbe and Vilmar. However, the theme was not given new importance and content until the middle of the century with the *affirmation of the Immaculate Conception as dogma* by Pius IX in 1854. Since that time it has met with both sharp repudiation and friendly agreement in close succession.

For example, the Prussian conservative theologian E. W. Hengstenberg was able to express far-reaching agreement with the new dogma. In 1853 he defended the doctrine and found that it offered no foothold for the 'divinisation of Mary'. Some years later the Protestant pastor W. O. Dietlein endeavoured to produce an appreciative evaluation of the dogma, which he did not regard as the expression of an extreme position, but rather as 'a careful elucidation of the conception which hitherto had been helplessly at the mercy of exaggeration and misunderstanding'. The very title of his little book *A Protestant Ave Maria* (1863) informs us of his intention to correct 'the grim and negative attitude' on the part of Protestantism to Mary.

Yet these impulses made but little headway; the stance of downright repudiation of the Roman Catholic development was more popular. For example, the *Protestantische Kirchenzeitung*, revived in 1854, violently contradicted such 'orthodox' utterances on the part of Protestants. One of its founders was *Kurt (von) Hase*, who as one of the first of the group, devoted a special chapter to Mary in his popular *Handbook of Protestant Polemic* (1862). His thoughtful Protestant rejection of the cult of the Madonna, marked by his learning and liberal openmindedness, was to prove typical and formative for the educated Protestant classes in the time preceding the First World War.

However, the weightiest intellectual opposition to the doctrine came from an 'orthodox' Lutheran; it is the impressive book of *Eduard Preuss Die römische Lehre von der unbefleckten Empfängnis aus den Quellen dargestellt und aus Gottes Wort widerlegt* (1865). After recounting the history of the dogma, the latter is investigated in the light of biblical and Reformation insights and evangelically 'tested' (after the manner of Martin Chemnitz's *Examen*, which Preuss had republished). The purpose of the author is to prove 'how unapostolic, how modern, this system is, which claims to be apostolic and ancient', and he comes to the conclusion that in modern Catholicism 'the old Christianity is lifted off its hinges, and a new religion has taken its place'. Such a committed approach in the spirit of the Reformation found, in fact, no support, and even its author did not remain true to it. However, in later times in Protestantism these two poles are to be found, warm appreciation and decided repudiation of Mariology.

Names worthy of mention on this theme are to be found repeatedly, in the circle of *advocates of a Protestant Mariology*. Before the First World War, the first name to be recorded is that of the north-German neo-orthodox theologian Emil Wacker with his book *Maria die Mutter des Herrn, oder Natur und Gnade* (1891). After the war it was Friedrich Heiler and his 'high church' circle who made many contributions to the discussion of the theme. Here, and in the Brotherhood of Saint Michael, for example in the work of Karl Bernhard Ritter, there are liturgical and ecumenical interests in the background. As an exegete Adolf Schlatter, the Tübingen professor and critic of the Lutheran Doctrine of justification, made a contribution with his *Marienreden* (1927). After the Second World War the discussion was resumed. The range of Protestant publications now extends from Friedrich Heiler and Wilhelm Stählin to Hans Asmussen (*Mary, the Mother of God* 1950) and Richard Baumann.

(ii) *Protestant Reaction to the Dogma of the Assumption*

An event of decisive importance was the proclamation of the dogma of the physical assumption of Mary into heaven by Pope Pius XII (1950). This dogmatic declaration elicited energetic *expressions of dissent* throughout the whole ecumenical field.

Friedrich Heiler collected these and developed them in his periodical *Oekumenische Einheit*. The most important Protestant expression of opinion in Germany is the *Evangelische Gutachten*, which the Heidelberg Theological Faculty has produced under the editorship of Edmund Schlink, and which formulates the profound misgivings of theologians who take their stand upon the Reformation.

The new dogma has significantly affected also the conversation between the confessions which since the papacy of John XXIII, is proceeding more intensively. Admittedly the Marian question, partly because of the reserve shown in the treatment of this theme by the Second Vatican Council, has clearly receded into the background in comparison with other themes (Orders, Eucharist, etc.). Yet everything indicates that the Marian theme has for some years been receiving increasing attention.

Not only are there more voices raised, and questions asked on the Catholic side; an entirely *new situation* seems to be arising under the pressures of a theology influenced or determined by feminist interests. Preliminary sketches of a theological and ecclesiastical treatment of the theme are offered by a group study by American Protestant and Catholic exegetes, and a paper of the Catholic Working Party of the United Evangelical-Lutheran Church in Germany (VELKD) *Maria, evangelische Fragen und Gesichtspunkte. Eine Einladung sum Gespräch* (1982). Yet the importance of the question is very far from being adequately acknowledged, and the beginnings of a Protestant answer are still very tentative.

3. CONTEMPORARY QUESTIONS AND POSSIBILITIES

(a) New Impulses

Thus, after a pause of thirty years, the Marian theme, if all appearances are not deceptive, is confronting the Protestant Church in an entirely new guise. Impulses are coming from different sides.

(i) Now they are coming from the side of *Catholic Ecumenism*. If Albert Brandenburg had earlier spoken of Luther's 'Marian theology', and, as it were, described Luther as a Mariologist, some time ago P. Gerhard Voss, OSB, drew the ecumenical consequences from this by stating that in fact Mary plays in the theology and piety of Protestant Christendom a smaller part than she might, or even ought to, on Protestant presuppositions. Recently the Bishop of Osnabrück has repeatedly suggested that Mary should be made the patroness of the Universal Church.

(ii) These thrusts have recently been reinforced by impulses on the part of a *feminist theology*. Originating in the United States it long ago reached Europe, and is to be found in all the great confessions, even if its forms vary. This means that even on the Protestant side 'Mary' has come in evidence in a new fashion, among the great complex of questions relating to the role of women in religion (Mary as symbol of the motherly element in God, etc.).

(iii) The old question raised by *liturgically interested 'high church'* or even '*catholicising*' Protestant theologians are not urgently raised at the present, yet they continue to be largely unsolved questions, which are today receiving new importance, especially from the spirituality of Protestant communities, in whose religious life Mary plays no small part (Darmstadt Sisterhood of Mary, Taizé, etc.).

Everything suggests that Protestantism is being challenged to deal more intensively with these questions, and to reply to them more in detail than it has done up to date. Protestant theology also will in the immediate future find itself no longer able to dispense with the theme of Mary in the customary fashion. Perhaps an 'ecumenical Mariology' is necessary for the future, if the mutual understanding of separated

Christians is to increase. The Protestant contribution to such an ecumenical doctrine of Mary cannot be one of enthusiastic approval of or mystical absorption in Catholic Mariology.

(b) Criteria for a Protestant Doctrine of Mary

In the strict sense *there cannot be a Protestant 'Mariology'* as an independent topic, because Mary has no value in herself, and can only be rightly seen in relation to her Son. A Protestant doctrine of Mary must therefore first of all be Christologically based and centred. Neither can the maximalist-Catholic programme *'De Maria nuquam satis'* (Of Mary enough can never be said), be a starting-point or guideline, nor a maximalist-feminist programme which places 'Woman' in the centre-point of religion.

Protestant theology must here find its *way between feminism and Catholicism*; its starting-point must be Holy Scripture, if it is to remain Protestant theology. Thus it would neither be Protestant nor would it be ecumenically profitable, if the Protestant contribution were not *biblical*. This is the place where contributions on the Protestant side have been inadequate, and the real exegetical treatment of the theme is only now beginning.

From this Protestant point of departure Mary can and must have a *place in preaching and proclamation*. Luther's exposition of the Magnificat can here serve as a magnificent example. This means that the figure of Mary is an occasion for us to praise the mighty acts of God. Finally, from a Protestant point of view, the theme of Mary cannot be left at the mercy of pious meditative extrapolation of thought or uncontrolled mythical thinking; it must not be withdrawn from the *critical control of theology*, otherwise one permits a rank growth of Mariology, 'i.e., an unwholesome growth of theological thinking. Unwholesome growths must be cut away' (Karl Barth).

By so doing theology takes in hand an important function of purification and avoidance of rank proliferation. *'Mary' must be defended from becoming the product of our pious imagination*. Religious need can never be a final criterion in Christian faith. In its search for a more biblically based conception of Mary, 'Protestant theology would have to be capable of making a worthwhile contribution not only to the Roman Catholic Church, but also to all the Christian confessions in the ecumenical conversation' (W. Völker). The most important fruit of a Protestant contribution might then well be, that behind the rank foliage of a mystical and uncontrolled 'Mariology', the real picture of our Lord's mother would be revealed in new astringency, simplicity and beauty.

Translated by David Cairns

The Most Important Literature

I.

Delius, Walter *Geschichte der Marienverehrung* (München/Basel 1963).
Graef, Hilda Maria *Eine Geschichte der Lehre und Verehrung* (Freiburg 1964).
Laurentin, René *Court Traité de Théologie Mariale* (Paris 1953).

II.

Düfel, Hans *Luther's Stellung zur Marienverehrung* (Gottingen 1968)
Ebneter, Albert 'Martin Luther's Marienbild'; *Orientierung* 20, 1956, 77ff. 85ff.
Meinhold, Peter 'Die Marienverehrung im Verständnis der Reformatoren des 16. Jahrhunderts' *Saeculum* 32, 1981, 43-58.
Schimmelpfennig, Reinhard *Geschichte der Marienverehrung im deutschen Protestantinismus*

(Paderborn 1952)
Tappolet, Walter *Das Marienlob der Reformatoren* (Tübingen 1962)
WA = *Weimarer Ausbage der Werke Luthers* (Weimar 1883 ff.).
Z = *Zwinglis Sämtliche Werke* (Berlin 1905 ff.).
CR = *Corpus Reformatorum*.

III.
Benko, Stephen *Protestanten, Katholiken und Maria* (Hamburg 1972).
Brandenburg, Albert *Maria in der evangelischen Theologie der Gegenwart* (Paderborn 1965).
Haselbarth, Hans 'Maria in der Frömmigkeit der evangelischen Kirche' *Una Sancta* 36 (1981) 371-423.
Heiler, Friedrich (ed.) *Evangelische Marienverehrung: Eine heilige Kirche* 1955-1956, volume I.
Lamparter, Helmut *Die Magd des Herrn* (Metzingen 1948, 1979²).
Mary in the New Testament. A Joint Study of Protestant and Catholic Theologians, under the Auspices of the United States Lutheran-Roman Catholic Dialogue, ed. Raymond Brown et al. (Philadelphia and New York 1978).
Miegge, Giovanni *The Virgin Mary. The Roman Catholic Marian Doctrine* (London 1955).
Mund, Hans-Joachim (ed.) *Maria in der Lehre von der Kirche* (Paderborn 1979).
Ruether, Rosemary Radford *Mary: The Feminine Face of the Church* (Philadelphia 1977).
Riesenhuber, Klaus *Maria im theologischen Verständnis von Karl Barth und Karl Rahner* (Quaestiones Disputatae 60. Freiburg 1973).
Max Thurian/Roger (Frère) *Maria, die Mutter des Herrn* (Mainz 1980).
Vischer, Lukas—'Maria Typus der Kirche und Typus der Menschheit' *Oekumenische Skizzen* (Frankfurt 1972) 115ff.
Völker, Werner 'Mariendogma und Marienverehrung im Dialog der Kirchen seit 1950' *Oekumenische Rundschau* 30 (1981) 1-19.
Several contributions in *Materialdienst des Konfessionskundlichen Instituts Bensheim*, the latest being 30 (1979) 65-69 (Horst Beinker); 32 (1981) 50-55 (Albert Mauder); 33 (1982) 84-89 (Jeiner Grote) and in the periodical *Una Sancta*.

Kari Børresen

Mary in Catholic Theology

A VAST area like Marian doctrine cannot be dealt with satisfactorily in so short an article, so I propose to treat it from one angle only, that of the interaction between theology and anthropology.[1]

Discourse about God and the relationship of God to mankind is determined by human experience in time and space. Theology, therefore, is always socio-culturally conditioned, and concepts of the divine are expressed by means of metaphors based on our variable human experience. At the same time, the way God is described affects the way mankind created in God's image is defined, and hence influences theological anthropology.

This interaction between theology and anthropology can be found in any Christian doctrine, but is particularly marked in discourse about Mary. In the course of the Church's history, Marian doctrine has been formulated from *three different points of view: the Christological, the ecclesiological and the Mariological.* This article will deal with each in turn.

1. CHRISTOLOGY: MARY GIVES BIRTH TO THE SON OF GOD

(a) Development of the doctrine

The great ecumenical councils only refer to Mary in Christological contexts. The first to mention her in its creed was not *Nicaea* (325), but *Constantinople* (381). Both these creeds were aimed at Arianism, according to which the Son was a creature of the Father, without pre-existence. The councils therefore had to affirm the Son's consubstantiality with the Father by eternal birth.[2]

The Council of *Ephesus* (431) focused attention on the Son's temporal birth. However, it opposed the patriarch of Constantinople, Nestorius, who, to preserve the distinction between the divine and human natures of the incarnate Son of God, favoured calling Mary *Kristotokos* (literally Christ-bearing). The patriarch of Alexandria, Cyril, countering Nestorius, preferred the term *theotókos* (God-bearing) in order to affirm the *unity* of the Son, who pre-existed by external birth and was given birth to *humanly* by Mary.[3] In the first anathema, he defined the word thus: the virgin is *theotókos*, for she brought forth after the flesh the Word of God who has become flesh.[4]

It is important to note, therefore, that in this controversy, the terms *Kristotokos* and *theotókos* had a physical and concrete meaning; they referred to the act of giving birth, not to motherhood in general. The word *mother (meter, mater)* was not used. Cyril was concerned to emphasise the *divine* character of the child given birth to *humanly* by Mary.[5]

The definition of faith drawn up by the Council of Chalcedon (451) explicated the term *theotókos* within this context of the two births by affirming the Son's *twofold* consubstantiality: with the Father by his divinity, and with us (understand: with Mary) by his humanity. Its stress on the Son's *unity* was to become standard: One and the same Christ, only-begotten Son, recognised in two natures, without confusion or division, subsisting in one person (*prosopon-hypostatis, persona-subsistentia*).[6]

The great scholastic theologians, such as Albert the Great, Bonaventure and Thomas Aquinas, defined the term *theotókos* (Latin *Dei genitrix*) in this perspective of the unity of the *persona*. The eternal birth thus implied divine fatherhood and, reciprocally, divine sonship. The temporal birth implied real motherhood on Mary's part, but did *not* reciprocally imply real sonship on the part of Christ, because although he was consubstantial with Mary by his humanity, the absence of human *persona* in the incarnate Son of God implied the absence of a *new* sonship in her regard.[7] When John Duns Scotus asserted *two* real sonships, the difference was terminological; he was attributing sonship, not to the divine *persona*, but to one of the two natures. Thus Mary's motherhood was real in the sense that it was a normal *physiological* function like that of any other human mother; Christ therefore really was her son. This interpretation was taken up by Francisco de Suárez at the end of the sixteenth century.

The terminology used is important in discourse about Mary. In the Greek tradition *theotókos* remained one of the main terms used to designate her, but in the Latin tradition there was a significant change: *Dei genitrix*, she who gives birth to God, was often replaced by *mater Dei*, the mother of God. This latter term occurs in the liturgy from the sixth century onwards, and in theology from the seventh (Ildephonsus of Toledo). But *Dei genitrix* remained the more frequent, and even when *mater Dei* did occur, e.g., in the scholastics, the two appear to be synonymous.

It should be noted that *conciliar* documents employed only terms with a physiological connotation, like *theotókos*, *Dei genitrix* and more specifically *Deipara* (*parere:* to give birth to), or again *mater Christi*, mother of Christ. The first council to use *mater Dei* was Vatican II, as a synonym for *genitrix Dei Filii*, she who gives birth to the Son of God, in the dogmatic constitution *Lumen gentium* (1964).[8]

(b) An androcentric view and its consequences

Classical Christology was expressed in accordance with the androcentric ideas of its day. It described Mary's part in the incarnation of Christ using an *androcentric gynæcology*, in which the father's role—filled in the case of Christ by the Holy Spirit—was seen as active, while the mother's role was passive. In this thought-pattern, the terms *theotókos* and *Dei genitrix* portrayed Mary as a receptacle at the time of conception, as gestatrix because she nourished the fœtus, and as parturient when she gave birth to the now viable child. The synonymous use of *mater Dei*, which presupposed an androcentric-type motherhood with the father's role as primary, carried the same implications.

The active-passive view was still current after the term 'divine' motherhood appeared in discourse on Mary, in the seventeenth century (Pierre de Bérulle). Mary's motherhood was considered 'divine' not because of its mode of operation, but by reason of its principle: the divinity of the Father eternally begetting the Son, and its end: the incarnate Son of God. Mary was still the *human* mother of a divine child.

The discovery of the mammalian ovule by Karl Ernst von Baer (1827) means that

E

Christology can no longer work with androcentric gynæcological presuppositions. If both parents have equivalent roles, then I would argue that to use the expression *mater Dei*, and *a fortiori* to speak of 'divine' motherhood, is to make Mary's role far more important than is compatible with the theocentrism of the great ecumenical councils.

The term *theotókos* which the councils used entails rejection of the old adage '*partus sequitur ventrem*' (the child has the status of the mother), since in this particular case, the Father and the incarnate Son share a common divinity. Furthermore, the expression 'divine' motherhood implies the converse formula, '*venter sequitur partum*' (the mother has the status of the child), in as much as Christ's divinity determines Mary's relation to him. Thus 'divine' motherhood, a basic principle of Mariology since the late nineteenth century (Matthias Joseph Scheeben), has now, with the titles 'mediatrix' and 'coredemptress', turned into what I like to call 'salvation gynaecology' (*Heilsgynäkologie*).

2. ECCLESIOLOGY: MARY, THE NEW EVE

The parallel drawn in Romans 5:14 between Adam and Christ: 'Adam was a figure (*typos*) of the one who was to come' inspired the theme of the new Eve which began to develop in the second century. For Justin (*Dialogue with Trypho* 100) and Irenæus (*Adversus haæreses* III, 22, 4; V, 19, 1), *Eve's disobedience at the fall* (Genesis 3:6) was counterbalanced by *Mary's obedience at the conception of the Son of God* (Luke 1:38). Tertullian for his part (*De anima* 43, 10) saw Eve's being formed from a rib of the sleeping Adam (Genesis 2:21-22), followed by his naming her the mother of all human beings (Genesis 3:20), as a figure of the Church being formed from the pierced side of the dying Christ (John 19:34). Originally, then, there were two separate parallels: one between *Eve and Mary*, the other between *Eve and the Church*.

Since Mary was likened to the Church, from the fourth century the two versions of the new Eve theme merged into one. In Ambrose, *both Mary and the Church are virgins and mothers* (*De institutione virginis* XIV, 88-89; *In Lucam* II, 7; 56-57). Augustine used the same comparison in his *De sancta virginitate* 2-6, treating Mary's faith in the context of the spiritual fecundity of the Church—the virgin wife of Christ—as mother (*mater ecclesia*). Mary, being a member of the Church, played a part in the Church's fecundity, having physically given birth to Christ, the head, whose members are born of the spirit. Elsewhere (*Sermo Denis* XXV, 7) he compares the two mothers but stresses that the Church is greater than Mary: she is a pre-eminent member of the Church but only a member nonetheless.[9]

The new Adam and new Eve typology extended to the whole of human history. At the creation, the first human couple prefigured Christ and the Church (Ephesians 5:31-32). Eve's role in bringing about the fall of Adam had its counterpart in Mary's role—that of receptacle—in the incarnation of the Son of God. Whereas Christ took flesh in the exemplary and normative sex of Adam, Mary represented the secondary, derived sex of Eve. As the redeemer, Christ is the new Adam, while the Church is the new Eve, his wife and helpmeet in the work of salvation. What this typology does, therefore, is to *transpose the androcentric system from the order of creation into the order of redemption*. It presupposes the socio-cultural patriarchal distinction between male and female roles, and then, within the typological couple, casts the human partner—Mary or the Church—in the instrumentally childbearing, i.e., specifically female role, and the divine partner, Christ, because of his pre-eminence, in the specifically male role.

Within the androcentric thought-pattern of the Fathers of the Church, to have the two partners figure in the order of redemption—as Adam and Eve had prefigured them in the order of creation—meant that salvation was guaranteed for women as well as men. Augustine explains this clearly (*De diversis quaestionibus* 83, 11): 'But the emancipation of man (*homo*) had to be shown in both sexes. Therefore, since it was fitting that he become man in the male sex, the more honourable one, it remained that the emancipation of the female sex should be seen in the fact that this man (*vir*) would be born of woman (*femina*).'[10]

Like the Scriptural texts it is based on (Hosea 2: 19-20; 2 Corinthians 11:2; Ephesians 5:31-32), the use of the new Adam and the new Eve theme for *nuptial* symbolism rests on the patriarchal assumption that marriage is a union between two unequal partners. In other words, the subordinate status of the wife is used as an analogy for human dependence on God. It is only to be expected that in a patriarchal culture, the Scriptural datum and the way it was interpreted should both be androcentric, and against such a background the symbolism is justifiable. But in today's world androcentrism is gradually breaking down, and with it, the socio-cultural background to the nuptial imagery, so that the symbolism is becoming void. I would argue that *the theme of the new Eve*, a historically conditioned human formulation, *is now an anachronism*, and that to go on using this anachronism is pernicious, because it helps to perpetuate ecclesial androcentrism.

3. MARIOLOGY: IMMACULATE CONCEPTION AND BODILY ASSUMPTION

As Christology and ecclesiology have their own proper objects, their discourse about Mary was relative and indirect. But with *the dogmatic definitions of 1854 and 1950*, Marian discourse became Mariological, i.e., it was directly concerned with Mary. Both these dogmas are based wholly on conjectural anthropological theories.

(a) The immaculate conception

The presupposition behind the idea of immaculate conception was the Augustinian doctrine of *original sin*, transmitted by paternal generation and leading to a contamination of the fœtus, the *infectio carnis*, which affected the rational soul at its infusion. Given the role of the Holy Spirit in his incarnation, Christ was exempt from this process. Mary's human condition had no Christological repercussions since in an androcentric biology, only the father actively engendered the child, so only the father transmitted original sin.

From the eighth century (John Damascene), it was considered fitting that, as Christ's mother, Mary should be purified of original sin. The great scholastics thought that she incurred the *infectio carnis*, since she was conceived in the normal human manner, but was then *sanctified* by means of a purifying intervention that occurred in two stages. The first stage took place in the womb, and according to Albert the Great and Bonaventure, happened just after animation. Thomas Aquinas did not specify the time. This stage consisted in her being freed from all actual sin, including venial sin. It should be noted that in the view of these doctors, who refer to Jeremiah 1:5 and Luke 1:15, Jeremiah and John the Baptist also were sanctified *in utero*, but only exempted from mortal sin. The second stage of Mary's sanctification occurred when Christ was conceived; at that point she was completely freed from original sin.

The idea of an intervention that actually prevented the *infectio carnis* arose in connection with the liturgical feast of Mary's conception; the feast was celebrated in England from the eleventh century, and spread on the Continent in the twelfth century. Several variants of this sanctification *in utero* were put forward, depending on the embryological theories adopted. Eadmer assumed that conception and animation were separated in time, and opted for a form of sanctification that prevented transmission of original sin at the moment of conception.[11] Nicholas of St Alban considered that the intervention occurred at infusion of the rational soul, and consisted in purification of the previously contaminated fœtal body. John Duns Scotus saw conception and animation as simultaneous; he thus combined the two views and put forward as the most likely thesis the idea of an intervention that preserved Mary from original sin at the moment of conception.

The council of Basel recognised this Marian privilege as early as 1493, but the council itself was considered invalid because of its conflict with Eugene IV. However, it is important to note the similarity between the formula used at Basel and the bull *Ineffabilis Deus* (8 December 1854). Both texts speak of a singular grace (*gratia singularis*) which preserved Mary untouched (*immunis*) by original sin by preventing it being transmitted to her at the time she would normally have contracted it. The emphasis the 1854 bull laid on *conceptio* clearly shows the influence of the Augustinian theory of original sin and presupposes the traditional connection between procreation and contamination.[12]

(b) The bodily assumption into heaven

The presupposition underlying the Marian doctrine of the Assumption was the notion of the *immortality of the rational soul*, a Platonic idea taken over by the Fathers of the Church. If death only affected the body, resurrection was resurrection of the *flesh*.

The liturgical feast of the dormition of Mary was introduced into the Roman Church at the end of the seventh century. The great scholastics treated the bodily assumption of Mary differently from her sanctification, accepting it as a pious belief. The same privilege of bodily assumption, it should be noted, was accorded to John the Evangelist, with reference to John 21:22-23. In the case of Mary, the reason given in support of the belief was its fittingness: *the idea that her body underwent decay after being separated from her soul at death could not be entertained.* The purifying or preserving sanctification she had been granted because of the role she played in the incarnation made it unthinkable that her body should putrefy in a grave. So its physical disintegration was prevented by having it reunited with her immortal soul immediately after her death. Her bodily assumption into heaven guaranteed that she would be present, body *and* soul, in the heaven of glory.

The scholastics only discussed *which part of the heavens Mary was in* after the assumption of her resurrected body. Albert the Great put her in the heaven of the creatures, with the higher angels. Thomas Aquinas thought she was above the angels, but below the abode of God. For Bonaventure, her place was in the heaven of the Trinity.

The traditional anthropological presupposition recurred in the apostolic constitution *Munificentissimus Deus* (1 November 1950). The duality of immortal soul and mortal body required a special intervention so that Mary's flesh could be saved the corruption of the grave and her separated soul be spared waiting for reunion with the risen body. Like the scholastics, then, the apostolic constitution appears to presuppose that Mary did actually die. However, given that death was the specific punishment for original sin, which according to the 1854 dogmatic statment Mary did not contract, the point is problematical. Some 'maximalist' theologians follow the logic through and assert that *Mary was exempted from the common law of mortality*.[13] This is still an open question. The 1950 formula, it should be pointed out, simply used the term *devicta morte* (death having been conquered) and so was fairly vague about this point. Nor did it specify the mode of Mary's bodily assumption or how it was related to her possible death; the privilege of assumption itself, however, was clearly aligned on the 1854 dogma and presented as a consequence of the immaculate conception.[14]

In their inspiration, both these dogmatic definitions were Mariocentric, since they were both the product of the nineteenth- and twentieth-century 'maximalist' Mariological movement. Moreover, given the traditional comparison between Mary and the Church, they also expressed ecclesial triumphalism. The 1950 dogma, however, can be seen in a Christological perspective, since it involves *a resurrection that looks forward to the fulfilment of all creation*, the exemplary cause of which is the resurrection of Christ. The 1854 dogma, by contrast, *attributed to Mary herself an exceptional place in the economy of redemption*.

Both the formulas are based on anthropological presuppositions which are now obsolete. I would argue that when the assumptions have been abandoned, the formulas lose all meaning and become literally incomprehensible. With the supporting structures—i.e., the Augustinian doctrine of original sin transmitted by paternal generation, or the classical doctrine of the immortality of the separated rational soul awaiting its risen body—cut from under them, these Mariocentric formulations are left hanging in the thin air of conjecture.[15]

4. THE RETURN TO ECCLESIOLOGY: *LUMEN GENTIUM*

By a vote of 1,114 to 1,074 the *Second Vatican Council* decided on 29 October 1963 to include its statement on Mary within the dogmatic constitution on the Church, *Lumen gentium*. This marked *the end of Mariology properly so-called* and *a return to an ecclesiological approach*.

The last chapter of *Lumen gentium* treated Mary *Deipara* within the mystery of Christ and the Church. The text is clearly Christocentric in intention; the functions it ascribes to Mary, using the patristic comparison between her and the Church, are *ecclesiotypical* (n. 53-61). This contrasts with the 1854 and 1950 dogmatic definitions in which, because of the parallels between Christ and Mary: supernatural conception and immaculate conception; ascension and assumption, Mary's privileges were Christotypical. The conciliar document attempts to situate Mary in a scriptural framework, and shows remarkable sobriety, particularly in comparison with the 'maximalist' trend in contemporary Mariological writing. The 1854 and 1950 formulas are used, but briefly and very discreetly (n. 53, 59, 62, 68). Mary is both a type of the Church on earth and the most eminent member of the eschatological Church (n. 63, 68).

Nevertheless, the text—which was finally approved by 1,996 votes to 23—was a compromise, and this is reflected in the *Christotypical inconsistencies* it contains. When it deals with Mary as the new Eve, it makes use of the patristic interpretations of Luke 1:38, but whereas for the early Fathers this text was about obedience and faith (n. 63), the council document uses *consentiens* and *cooperans* (consenting and co-operating n. 56; cf. 58 with reference to John 25:19), and so reads more into Luke's text.[16] Other passages reflect the 'maximalist' hankering after the idea of Mary as mediator and co-redeemer. She is called a generous collaborator (*generosa socia*) and described as suffering with (*compatiens*) and thus co-operating in (*cooperata est*) the salvific work of the dying Christ (n. 61). Again with reference to Luke 1:38, she is viewed as *mediatrix* (62), which clashes with the Christocentric idea of the one mediator affirmed in n. 60.

As far as was feasible, then, *Vatican II encouraged the 'minimalist' line in Marian thinking* only fourteen years after the dogma of the Assumption was defined. The council's attitude was a result of the return to patristic sources that has characterised Catholic theology in the twentieth century. *Lumen gentium* marked an advance because it returned to the ecclesiological view of Mary. But its use of the traditional sources was still dominated by the androcentric assumptions of the early Fathers; the new Eve was still a projection of the patriarchal mind. The female still represented humankind in its subordinate relation to the male, Christ.

5. MARY AFTER VATICAN II

(a) Mary, mother of the Church

In his speech promulgating *Lumen gentium* on 21 November 1964, Paul VI proclaimed Mary *mater ecclesiae* (mother of the Church). The Polish bishops had launched the idea of this title at the council, and John XXIII wanted it to be conferred, but the doctrinal commission which prepared the chapter on Mary had rejected it. It set Mary above the Church and so was a departure from the patristic theme of *ecclesia mater* (the Church as mother). By promulgating it, therefore, Paul VI turned his back on the ecclesiotypism of *Lumen gentium*. Originally, this title was given to the Holy Spirit; it was only rarely used of Mary, by Latin writers from the twelfth century on. Since Vatican II, it has often been applied to Mary in pontifical documents, to the reassurance of those theologians who are still 'maximalist'. It is a Christotypical title, since it implies that Mary played a part in the redemption.

(b) Mary, a figure of liberation

Liberation theology, which sprang up in South America where it doubtless meets a need, sees Mary as a figure of God's creation set free by Christ. In the context of the *Magnificat* (Luke 1:44-55), it is Mary who proclaims the liberation of the poor and the oppressed. Traditionally, she has been greatly venerated in South American Catholicism; now, she has become the herald of the new order. Liberation theology seems well suited to the particular socio-political background, but one should not forget that this makes it all the more a product of circumstances. *If the actual liberator is Christ, not Mary, I see no reason why liberation theology should not remain Christocentric.*

(c) Mary, a feminist model

It is understandable that Catholic feminists should value the only female model available in traditional doctrine (often more shrewdly than their non-Catholic sisters). Nevertheless there is a serious flaw in their position: this feminist Mary is rooted in androcentric typology; she is therefore a contradiction of feminism. To make Mary a model for feminists is not only questionable but also absurd, if the essential ecclesiological and Mariological connection between femininity and subordination is ignored or not known. The new Eve theme cannot be used in the struggle for women's liberation precisely because of this asymmetry. It may push Mary to the limits of the human, but her partner remains divine. More, this symbolism is harmful, because it prevents Christian women from tackling the central problem of how to overcome the androcentric convergence of Scripture and tradition.

(d) Mary, the feminine dimension of God

In doctrine, Mary is human, with privileges that are the result of redemption by Christ. But in folklore, she occupies part of the area left vacant by the old mother-goddesses; this is an important aspect of popular religion. Discourse that presents Mary as the feminine dimension of God feeds on this folklore, but thereby moves outside the field of doctrine.[17] For me, this conception of Mary is, in the strict sense of the term, a deviation, and all the more noxious because some feminists are pacified by it. As against this, however, the theme of the feminine dimension of God can help to show the need for feminine metaphors in discourse about God. If both woman *and* man are made in God's image, *God must be feminised, i.e., feminine as well as masculine terms* must be used in the human expression of God we call theology.[18] Approaching the problem by divinising Mary, on the other hand, is heretical.

6. THE ECUMENICAL PERSPECTIVE: A RETURN TO CHRISTOLOGY

Although the post-conciliar trends discussed above have been distinctly 'maximalist', I expect future developments to follow through from the return to ecclesiology initiated by *Lumen gentium*, and show a return to Christology. This expectation is based on the fact that Catholic theology, which has been renewed since the end of the nineteenth century by its return first to scholastic and then to patristic sources, is now in the middle of a return to scriptural sources.

The main problem with Catholic discourse about Mary is *the disparity between the biblical data and the doctrinal interpretation put on it*. The principle of fittingness has repeatedly been used in the history of theology to produce an accumulation of Marian prerogatives. The resulting gap between the Mary of Scripture and the Mary of doctrine can easily be done away with by a Christological approach, in which it is only in Christ that the divine is made concretely manifest in the human. *Mary will thus be stripped of her Christological attributes*.

The *androcentric presuppositions* which the great ecumenical councils operated with *are now unusable* for expressing our faith in the Trinity and the incarnation of the Son of God. When the pre-eminence of the divine is no longer pictured by male metaphors, and human dependence on God is no longer shown in terms of female subordination to the male, *the ecclesiotypical attributes of Mary will also disappear*. Jesus' historical sex will lose the androcentric significance it had in patristic typology. The figure of Mary will stop being a patriarchal construct: virgin, wife and mother, an adjunct to the male.

The disappearance of patriarchal forms of society is a challenge to the fundamental androcentrism of Catholic doctrine; we need a *new* theology. However, from the ecumenical point of view, this androcentrism in theocentric guise is an advantage, since the subordination of the female element in the economy of salvation means that Mary's position is not as elevated as even 'maximalist' expressions of it appear to suggest. When the androcentric assumptions that underlie them have broken down, it will become impossible to use the traditional terms for Mary or the Church. *Theotókos* or *mater ecclesia* will no longer have connotations of female dependence and so will not be applicable, since to use them in a post-patriarchal society would raise the status of the human to an extent that is irreconcilable with the primacy of the divine.

From the ecumenical point of view, the fact that among Catholics there are real 'variations'[19] about Mary is important. The Catholicism of my own background is atypical, since it is Scandinavian, is a minority religion, and gives very little, if any, attention to Mary; in no way then do I represent the traditional attitude found in 'Catholic' countries. Faced with Mary as she is venerated in southern Italy or Poland, I am alienated. *Differences of attitude towards Mary seem to me to be determined more by socio-cultural than by confessional background*. In this respect, the coincidence of Mariocentrism with national economic weakness is striking, as is the connection between devotion to Mary and male chauvinism. This socio-Mariology, as I call it, could be an important research field, and would probably cross the confessional divide.

Translated by Ruth Murphy

Notes

In notes 2, 3, 4 and 6, the abbreviation *COD* stands for *Conciliorum œcumenicorum decreta* (Bologna 1972).

1. For exhaustive and sober studies of the field, see the works of R. E. Brown on Mary in Scripture and R. Laurentin on Mary in doctrine.

2. *COD* 5, 24.

3. Correspondence between Cyril and Nestorius *COD* 44, 47, 58.

4. *COD* 59.

5. For concern with Mary in Egyptian circles at Cyril's time, see *Apophthegmata patrum* in which Mary is only mentioned *once*, and then as *theotókos* (*Patrologia graeco-latina* 65, 358 (n. 144)).

6. *COD* 86.

7. For the different aspects of scholastic discussion of Mary, see my book *Anthropologie médiévale et théologie mariale* (Oslo 1971).

8. See n. 57, 61, 63, 69 = *Deipara*; n. 66, 67 = *Dei genitrix*; n. 66, 69 = *mater Dei*.

9. 'Sancta Maria, beata Maria, sed melior est ecclesia quam virgo Maria. Quare? quia Maria portio est ecclesiae, sanctum membrum, excellens membrum, supereminens membrum, sed tamen totius corporis membrum' *Miscellanea Agostiniana* I (Rome 1930) 162.

10. *Corpus Christianorum* 44 A (Turnholti 1975) 18.

11. The principle of fittingness is transposed to the level of the divine will: 'Potuit plane. Si igitur voluit, fecit' *Tractatus de conceptione sanctae Mariae* ed. H. Thurston, T. Slater (Freiburg Br. 1904) 11.

12. *Enchiridion Symbolorum* (Freiburg Br. 1965) 561-562.

13. See M. Jugie 'La Mort et l'assomption de la sainte Vierge' *Studi e Testi* 114 (Vatican City 1944) 569-582. Pius XII is said to have held this view.

14. *Enchiridion Symbolorum* 781-782.

15. See *op. cit.* note 7, 116-119.

16. The interpretation of Luke 1:38 to mean active consent dates from the beginning of the eighteenth century (L.-M. Grignion de Montfort).

17. See A. Greeley *The Mary Myth: On the Femininity of God* (New York 1977); L. Boff *Il volto materno di Dio* (Brescia 1981). Note that this shift from mother of God to Mother God is found in L. A. Feuerbach *Des Wesen des Christentums* (1841) (Leipzig 1923) pp. 95-104.

18. See my articles 'Christ notre mère, la théologie de Julienne de Norwich' *Mitteilungen und Forschungsbeiträge der Cusanus-Gesellschaft* 13 (Mainz 1978) 320-329; 'L'Usage patristique de métaphores féminines dans le discours sur Dieu' *Revue théologique de Louvain* 13 (Louvain 1982) 205-220; 'God's Image, Man's Image? Female Metaphors describing God in the Christian Tradition' *Temenos* 19 (Helsinki 1983)

For papal efforts in this direction, see John Paul I *Angelus*, 10 September 1978 (Isaiah 49:15); *Lo spazio di un sorriso* ed. P. Beretta (Rome 1978) 70 John Paul II 'Dives in misericordia' 30 November 1980, notes 52 (Isaiah 49:15); 61 (Luke 1:72) *Acta Apostolicae Sedis* 72 (Rome 1980) 1190, 1193.

19. See Bossuet *Histoire des variations des Eglises protestantes*, 1688.

PART III

New Impulses

Virgil Elizondo

Mary and the Poor:
A Model of Evangelising Ecumenism

INTRODUCTORY NOTES

(a) The fact of Marian Devotion

IT IS an undeniable fact that devotion to Mary is the most popular, persistent, and original characteristic of Latin American Christianity. It stands at the origins of Christianity in the New World. From the very beginning, her presence has given dignity to the downtrodden, hope to the exploited and motivation to all the liberation movements.[1] Regardless of the interpretation, the fact of the massive devotion to Mary cannot be denied.

(b) Key to proper interpretation: Cosmovision of Pre-Columbian Mesoamerica

In seeking to understand the theological meaning of this devotion, one must study it through its own proper origins and function in the salvific process of Latin America. Studying it through the Mariological practices and theologies of the West will lead to misunderstanding and error. Such a process would impose a meaning that would not correspond to the true meaning which it has for the people. Hence I beg readers conditioned by Western thought to put aside their very legitimate presuppositions and to take a fresh look at a theological reality that is totally different from anything in the Western tradition.[2]

(c) Limitation and objective

I will not attempt to study Marian devotion throughout Latin America because it would take a much longer study to do it justice. Hence, I will concentrate on devotion to Our Lady of Guadalupe at Tepeyac. This devotion stands at the very origins of Mexican Christianity and has developed from being the Lady of the Indians, to being the first Lady of Mexico, to being declared the Patroness of Latin America by the popes, and today is rapidly being recognised by more and more people from Canada to Argentina as the Mother of the Americas—North and South. In this article, I will develop the thesis that the apparition of Our Lady of Guadalupe in 1531 together with the subsequent devotion of the people is a major disclosure in the ongoing growth and development of the Christian understanding of God.

1. HISTORICAL ORIGINS OF MEXICAN CHRISTIANITY

Violence, rape, and death marked the birth of Latin America. The Christian European invasion beginning at the end of the 1400s initiated a process of extermination, enslavement and exploitation of such an extent and duration that it is difficult to find similar parallels in history. The aftermath of these events is not just history but continues to grow and deepen in today's world.

The violence was multiple and all-embracing: the brutality of the conquest, the degrading rape of the native women, the imposition of a totally New World order of the Spanish crown (Portuguese in Brazil), and the attempts to discredit and destroy the ultimate root of the people's life: their religion. While the new colonial rule reduced all the natives to insignificant and inferior human beings whose very humanity had to be debated and who appeared to be destined to be the servants and slaves of the white invaders, the missioners tried to impose belief in a God that was totally foreign and alienating to the native people. The God they presented was the eternal male judge who was anxious in his justice to punish the faults of men and women. Thus, the Spaniards were the arm of God sent to punish the infidelities and wrongdoings of the Indians.

Missionary effort proceeded by way of radical opposition: the *Christian religion versus the religion of others*. If the Christian God had conquered in battle, now the same God must claim the total allegiance of the newly conquered people. All traces of their 'pagan' and 'diabolical' practices had to be irradicated.

The missioners were great men of the gospel. They struggled even at the cost of their own lives to protect and defend the Indians. They truly loved the natives and tried to help them. Nevertheless, they themselves were agents of the ultimate violence which religion alone is capable of inflicting.

The conquest and missionary efforts resulted in the institutionalisation of a four-fold oppression.

A *political-economic* one through the imposition of a new form of living and of government in favour of the powerful and to the detriment of the conquered.

A *sexual one* because of the violation of the native women. Even the native men would begin to follow the model of the conquistador: abuse the women and leave them along with the children.

A *socio-psychological one* because the conquered Indian—even the nobles and wisemen of the native people—would be reduced to a permanent status of servitude and inferiority. They were henceforth to listen, learn, and obey the new masters They were rendered silent and defenceless.

Finally it would be a *religious oppression* because the God-agents of the new power would battle fiercely for the total eradication of the native religions. What they could not understand, they would approach as diabolical. They would give their lives to defend the Indians as children of God. But at the same time, they would deny the Indians the ultimate root of existence. Even as the natives and the mestizos have become Christians, the religious oppression continues because their faith expressions have been labelled and interpreted for them by the Western élites, but they themselves have never been asked to be active partners in the theologising process proper to the new and developing local church.

2. UNSUSPECTED IRRUPTION

It is within the context of death and despair that a divine irruption takes place far away from the centres of power of the State or of established religion. It was *the apparition of the Indian Queen of Heaven to* a poor Indian named *Juan Diego* in the periphery of Mexico City. Through this happening, millions of Indians regained their dignity and their desire to live. Today, over 450 years later, the devotion continues to grow and develop. Through it the millions of oppressed poor people continue to find life, security, and hope.[3]

Out of *Tepeyac Hill* (site of the ancient sanctuary of the maternal aspect of the deity under the name of *Tonantzin*) music and song (Nahuatl image indicating a divine revelation) announce the beginning of a new day. Juan Diego climbed to the top of the hill (Nahuatl priests climbed to the top of the pyramid to become the mediators between the divine and the human) where he saw a beautiful Lady whose dress radiated like the sun (the Nahuatl glyph for God; therefore in Nahuatl thought, a lady that radiated divinity because her innermost being was divine). She presents herself as *'ichipohtli Sancta María . . . Inninantzin inhuelnelli teotl Dios'*. The Indian narrative continues utilising many of the traditional Nahuatl expressions for God.

In essence her message is, 'Know and understand that I am the ever-Virgin Holy Mary, Mother of the true God through whom one lives: the Creator, the Lord of the Near and the Togetherness, the Lord of Heaven and Earth.' In the original Nahuatl narrative it is immediately evident that there is a new discourse about God which *unites not just the Spanish and the Nahuatl languages but equally the Nahuatl understanding of God with the Spanish one.* The very expression of God which the missioners had tried desperately to wipe out as diabolical is now combined with Spanish expressions of God which the Indians had found incomprehensible. The entire account is presented in the Nahuatl context of a divine intervention and revelation.

The results of the new expressions of God and of the Mother of God are an amazing enrichment of the very understanding of the selfhood of God. *It is no longer the European expression of God nor the Nahuatl expression of God but a new mestizo expression* which is mutually interpretive and enriching. No longer will there be radical opposition between the two religions. As the genes and the chromosomes of the parents which join to produce a new baby, the core elements of two religions were united to produce a new one which would be alienating of neither and complementary to both. After many unsuccessful attempts on the part of the missioners, a new possibility for true and mutually enriching religious dialogue was now made possible.

Juan Diego, a scorned Indian, who had been on his way to church to learn about things divine is now addressed in a most dignified, personal and tender way by the *Mother of the Creator and of our Saviour.* She states that she has many servants and messengers that she could send. It is important to note that the Spanish presented themselves as the chosen servants and messengers of the true God. But the Lady of Heaven states that it is in every way precise that Juan Diego, her especially loved and esteemed one, be her personal messenger so that through his mediation her will might be accomplished.

This does not deny the function of the missioner, but it does reverse the function of the Indian. As the Spaniards were missioners to the Indians, the Indians are now commissioned to be missioners to the Spaniards. The *Indians* would no longer be just passive recipients, but *active agents in the construction of the new religion.* It would no longer be a question of masters and subjects but one of equal partners in a common enterprise. In the person of Juan Diego, the conquered and despised Indians now become the chosen vessels and teachers of the new way of love. It is through the Indian efforts that the Bishop, eventually the officialdom, and today even Rome, have accepted the new American incarnation of the gospel.

'I vividly desire that a temple be built on this site, so that in it I can present and give all my love, compassion, help and defence, for I am your most pious mother . . . to hear your laments, and to remedy all your miseries, pains and sufferings.' While the missioners were labouring to build a new church according to the best of their own Spanish mind[4] but which in effect justified the conquest with its new socio-political world order and cosmovision, the message of the Lady would produce a radical change and be the basis for the on-going struggles for justice which continue to this day. The new temple (the Nahuatl glyph indicating a world order with its cosmovision) would be the sign of the constant struggle against injustice, misery, rejection and insult. *It was not New Spain, but the New Temple which the Lady of Heaven wanted for the Americas of the future.* In it the Mother of the God of ultimate truth (another Nahuatl expression of God) was offering not punishment but compassion, love, and defence.

3. TOWARDS A THEOLOGICAL INTERPRETATION

Throughout the Bible, the manifestation of *the divine is always in function of the liberation of the oppressed*. Because the Israelites were the rejected and ridiculed of the world, their experience and perception of being God's chosen people was the deepest root of their sustained dignity and their struggles for liberation. The Guadalupe event functions in the same way. Many have tried to manipulate and 'spiritualise' it so as to take away the fullness of the liberating impact. Nevertheless, it has not been lost. The Virgin of Guadalupe has been the banner that has led the wars of independence and the movements of revolution and reform in Mexico. Today in the United States it animates the farmworker movement in its struggles for justice. The people very spontaneously refer to Mary as Queen, Virgin, Defensor and Protectress, and Mother. As used by the people, these titles arise out of the Guadalupe narrative and its function in the struggles of the Mexican Christians. They clearly express the role of Mary in the salvific process of Mexico.[5]

The Guadalupe event is the beginning of the four-fold liberation of the people.

(a) Political-economic liberation

As the conqueror imposed a new political-economic order of exploitation, despotism and deprivation which was solidly anchored on and justified by the divinely established order of the supremacy of the Catholic Kings of Spain and the Supreme Pontiff in Rome, *the new Queen of Tepeyac would inaugurate a new order of life* which would be the basis for the reversal of the evils of the conquest. She would not conquer through physical force or threat of eternal punishment but through her everloving presence and compassion. She will remedy their miseries by leading them in their struggles. She will alleviate their pains by bringing healing out of the newly imported diseases. She will be the true Queen (versus the Kings of Spain) of all the inhabitants of this land.

(b) Liberation from sexual violation

The sexual oppression is countered by the appearance of the ever-Virgin Mary, Mother of God and our Mother. In this case *virginity is in opposition to the scandal and shame of violated womanhood*. She was pure and unsoiled because she had not been touched by the raping hands of the conquistador. In her, Mexican womanhood is restored to its original dignity. Equally is the Mexican male liberated for no longer will he have to suffer the castrating effects of seeing his beloved women violated and not being able to do anything about it. What has been prostituted and abused by the conquistador is now virginised by God. In this case, virginity is the complete rehabilitation of abused personhood.

The Virgin Mother of Tepeyac does not militate against humanising sexual relationships. She counters the insulting and dehumanising effects of the rape and abuse of oppressed women and the destructive shame it equally casts upon its men. Even if poor women are forced into prostitution by the structures of oppression, they are kept virginally pure by the all-protecting Virgin Mother.

(c) Socio-psychological Liberation

The apparition is also a liberation from the socio-psychological oppression because she will *listen to the silenced poor*, she will call them by name, and place all her confidence in them. In the person of Juan Diego their crushed dignity is restored and from their imposed worthlessness, they are called upon to be the chosen servants and messengers. The Empire would condemn them to a perpetual status of minors—not even allowing them into sacred orders and certainly not listening to their ideas or opinions. Yet the Mother of God would listen to them, constitute them as her trusted messengers, and be ever present to protect and defend them.

(d) Religious liberation

Finally, it is a liberation from the religious oppression. *An exclusively male God could never be comprehended or accepted.* In the Nahuatl cosmovision, everything which is perfect has a male and a female component: the cosmos, creation, the human person and God. These two aspects are not contradictory but complementary. *As the paternal aspect of God is the all-powerful creator and giver of life, the maternal aspect, typified by Mary of Tepeyac, is the all-powerful suppliant.*

The mother listens to the cries of her children and takes their petitions to the Father who cannot deny them because it is the mother who is asking. But beyond this the Mother does not just ask, it is she who initiates all new endeavours. Hence the Father does not just give what the Mother asks for, but he brings to fruition what the mother initiates. It is in this sense that the ancient *Ometecuhtli-Omecihuatl*[6] complex is now discovered in the earthy ever-Virgin Mary. The feminine aspect is added to the God of the Christians while the personal is added to the God of the Indians in a profound enrichment of both! There is here a redemptive and expanding mutuality of both religions which results in the new Christianity of Mexico . . . of the Americas.

The supreme gift of this 'earth-asking' Mother and 'heaven-giving' Father is Jesus of Nazareth who comes to give his life for the sake of the new creation. The narrative refers to the Saviour and at the very centre of the Guadalupe image—right over the womb—is the Nahuatl symbol for the centre of the universe. Through her, the Lord will become incarnated deeply into the cultural soil of the New World. Out of this incarnation of the gospel, a new church will be born which will be neither the restoration of the ancient pre-Colombian religions nor the mere imposition of the imported church of the conquerors.

CONCLUSION

Guadalupe introduced an evangelising process that is of its very nature ecumenical because it brings about dialogue at the level of our image of God. The Guadalupe event initiates such a dialogue. The result has been the beginning of a new religious unity which would neither alienate the zealous missioners of Western Christianity nor deprive the natives of Mexico of their deepest treasure. It is indeed *the beginning of Mexican Christianity* through the process of evangelising ecumenism: new life and unity no longer by way of eradication but by way of synthesis.

As Hellenised Christianity opened new horizons for the universal understanding of Christianity, so *Mexican Christianity today opens exciting new possibilities* for the universal development in our understanding of God and ways of God. But to enter this new adventure, one must proceed through the ways of thought of the oppressed poor of the New World. God is faithful to God's way and thus continues to guide us to the fullness of truth through the little ones of the world: 'At that moment Jesus rejoiced in the Holy Spirit and said: "I offer you praise, O Father, Lord of Heaven and Earth, because what you have hidden from the learned and the clever you have revealed to merest children'" (Luke 10:21).

The theological structures of the West have kept the theologians of Europe and of the Americas from fully understanding the creativity of Guadalupe.[7] This privilege has been reserved to the masses of the faithful poor who patiently tolerate the rituals, the sermons and the theological discourses of the God-agents of the dominant culture while they persevere *in the new way of the Mother of Our Lord of Heaven and Earth*. The Marian devotion of the poor leads the universal Church to a new appreciation of the very selfhood of God. We cannot say exactly what it will be. We can only point to it and begin to suspect what it might be.

It is only when the silenced, ignored and ridiculed Indians, Mulattos and Mestizos, began to speak freely about the inner meaning of their faith experience that the full theological implications of Marian devotions will be known by the rest of the Christian world. It is they who will come forth with the new theological tradition of the New Church which has incarnated in the cultural soil of the new world of the Americas. As the East and the West have had their traditions, so will the New World. God's poor will lead us into unsuspected and fascinating disclosures into the very mystery of God.

Notes

1. In a symposium which I conducted in the Instituto Catequistico Latino Americano in Manizales, Colombia in 1977, it was evident that the chief Mariological devotion of each Latin American country represented stood at the very beginnings of that country and equally that it was a liberating experience for the downtrodden of that country.

2. As Western cultures have elaborated and deepened our understanding of the Word, so are other cultures capable of doing so today. Consult: *Lumen Gentium, Ad Gentes.,* and *Nostra Aetate* of Vatican II and John Paul II's address to the Pontifical Biblical Commission of 26 April 1979.

3. For a full discussion of the Guadalupe apparition and its interpretation consult: V. Elizondo *La Morenita: Evangelizer of the Americas* (San Antonio 1980) and 'Our Lady of Guadalupe as a Cultural Symbol: "The Power of the Powerless"' in *Concilium* 102 (1977) 25-33; C. Siller 'Para una teología del Nican Mopohua' in *Servir* 62 (1976) 155-174; and 'El Metodo de la evangelización en el Nican Mopohua' in *Servir* 93-94 (1981) 255-293.

4. For a discussion of the heroic positive efforts of the missioners, consult Enrique Dussel *A History of the Church in Latin America: Colonialism to Liberation* (Grand Rapids 1981); also consult the historical collection which is emerging out of CEHILA in Latin America.

5. M. Velasquez 'El fenomeno social del guadalupanismo' *Servir* (1976) 123-154.

6. M. Leon-Portilla *La Filosofia Nahuatl* (Mexico 1974).

7. Judeo-Christian theology has focused exclusively on the metaphor of God's paternity even to the point of ignoring the maternal-feminine face of God which also appears in the biblical tradition. In the very masculine-feudal middle ages a strong Marian devotion had a certain impact on Catholic popular devotion. The question is, however, whether this medieval Marian devotion ever led to a new thinking about God which would have revitalised certain biblical feminine aspects of the God of History.

F

Catharina Halkes

Mary and Women[1]

IT IS hardly possible to provide a complete picture, in such a short article, of what is said about Mary—I could almost say here: of what happens to Mary—when feminist theologians reflect about her person and her significance. This article may therefore be thought of as a glimpse into the workshop of a feminist theologian who has gradually come to a deeper insight into what should be taking place when the mystery and the symbol of Mary are understood more fully. I shall not, in other words, say anything about *the* feminist theology with regard to Mary. All that this article claims to be is an interim report of a quest for the significance of Mary not only for women, but also for men. One result of this may perhaps be that Christian faith in this regard will lose some of its ambiguities.

I am very aware of the fact that the image of Mary will not produce unanimous reactions among feminist theologians who are working with an up-to-date theology or among ordinary Christians at the level of popular piety. It is precisely because Mary is a woman that a link is made between her and women which can easily lead to uncritical conclusions. A frequent result of this is that Mary is ultimately rejected by feminist theologians as a possible symbolic identification figure.

I, however, have consciously chosen to continue to be concerned with this figure. I can give at least five main reasons for this:

(*a*) It is important to set Mary free from the image that has been made of her and from the projections attached to her by a male and priestly hierarchy. It is because of a deep sense of solidarity or sisterhood that I do not want simply to let go of Mary.

(*b*) Women have to be liberated from the still prevalent images of Mary which limit women. Those images have therefore to be analysed and exposed.

(*c*) A feminist criticism should also be heard in the new theological reflections that are now gaining ground, so that this may lead to a possible new approach. There are still many male theologians who quite blandly write about Mary and femininity without taking the experiences that are expressed by women themselves into account.

(*d*) Mary is still a stumbling block in ecumenical dialogue, but feminist theology has points of departure which make it primarily ecumenical in its aims and intentions. It has therefore to take part in this often difficult dialogue.

(*e*) My last reason is a personal one. I find the complex problem that emerges as soon as Mary is studied more closely quite fascinating. I would venture to suggest that the figure of Mary is more suitable than any other figure for the purpose of bringing to light the very ambivalent position of the Church and its theologians with regard to human sexuality in general and that of women in particular. It can also be used to show which models of conversion and which mechanisms have been applied to make Mary an impossible model, which is used against women, which is not in any way critical of men, and which legitimises the gap that has been allowed by the Church to persist between (female) sexuality and the mediation of holiness.

I regard it as very important that these themes should be critically examined. Although it is not possible in this article to discuss each one separately, I have kept them firmly in mind.

1. MARY AS A HISTORICAL AND SYMBOLIC FIGURE

What we know about the figure of Mary comes from the gospels. Although her roots are in the Bible, it has to be admitted that she has no clear form in Scripture and that she does not have what might be called a clear face. She is the mother of Jesus of Nazareth, but the evangelists are concerned with the proclamation of Jesus as the Messiah, whose natural mother and brothers are outlined or at least relativised over and against the *familia Dei* (see Mark 3:31-35). Luke counts Mary as one of those who hears and carries out the Word of God, but it is in his gospel that we find Jesus' statement about the blessed state of biological motherhood, that is, bearing and feeding (Luke 11:27-28), being critically adapted to the dignity of discipleship. It is, moreover, well known that the two infancy narratives in Matthew and Luke were later additions to the gospels, included because it was felt necessary to reflect in faith about the mystery of the incarnation. In Luke especially, these chapters provide a very lively account, culminating in the two encounters (with the angel and with Elizabeth) and with the two key-words *fiat* and *magnificat*.

A concrete, historical Mary hardly appears at all in the gospel of John. She only occurs in two scenes, and the scene at the foot of the cross is increasingly regarded now as a case of theological symbolism, the mother and the disciple together representing the *ecclesia*.

It is valuable, then, to recognise that, although Mary, the mother of Jesus, was a historical figure with her roots in the Bible, she was also a symbolic figure in the tradition of the Church. As Pannenberg has suggested, Mariological ideas belong more to symbolic themes than to scholastic and conceptual thought.

This has been expressed in a different way by Wolfhart Pannenberg. He has said that the most important difference between Christology and Mariology is methodological. Christology is an explicitation of the significance of a historical event, whereas Mariology attempts to personify the characteristics of the new humanity in Mary. Following Justin Martyr (Dial. 100, 4), Irenaeus claimed that Mary was the representative of the whole of humanity and contrasted the (disobedient) Eve with the (obedient) Mary. This too is an expression of the symbolic aspect of Mary.

For the sake of clarity, I would like to stress here that I do not regard a symbolic figure as in any sense less important than a historical one, certainly not when the most profound levels of the human soul are involved—in other words, at the religious level. Here, however, we are concerned with two different data, values or revelations. This fact leads me to conclude that, if we are to do justice to the various ways of looking at Mary—as virgin, bride and mother, as the queen of heaven or as the comforter of those who mourn, for example—it is not enough to turn to theology. It is necessary to include the findings of comparative religion and religious and depth psychology.

2. THE MARY OF THE CHURCH'S TEACHING
AND THE MARY OF POPULAR PIETY

Doctrines

The fundamental problem is how to look at the history of devotion to Mary throughout the whole of the history of the Church. The Church's magisterium has solemnly declared that Mary is the *theotókos* (Ephesus, 431 A.D.) and the *Dei parthenos* (Lateral Synod of 649), that she is exempt from original sin (the dogma of 1854) and that she has been taken up into heaven (the dogma of 1950). From the theological point of view, it is clear that three of these four dogmas have a Christological content and point to the mystery of Christ and that the fourth expresses man's fulfilled redemption.

On the one hand, then, a truth of faith concerning Christ is revealed and established through Mary. What is expressed, in other words, is that he really became man and was born of a human mother and that his birth was the result of a divine initiative, taking place outside the sphere of sexual union and through a woman who had been previously exempted from original sin for the sake of the one who was born of her. On the other hand, Mary symbolises the ultimate salvation of all mankind. Mary is therefore never seen in isolation—she is always a reference to something or to someone else. We are therefore bound to ask: who is Mary herself?

Even as early as Ephesus, Mary took the place of the goddess Diana and gave form to the mystery of the divine mother that was so indispensable to men. Gradually two Marys began to emerge. The first of these is the Mary of the Church's teaching, in which great care has always been taken to ensure that her person remains subordinate to that of Christ so that her lustre will not outshine that of Christ and in which Mary owes her excellence entirely to God's grace and the birth of Christ. The second Mary is the figure at the centre of increasing and sometimes excessive piety, usually of a popular kind, but also including that of such male theologians as St Bernard. That piety has a radiating effect and acts evocatively. It is the result of a deep-seated need on man's part for what will give, nourish and sustain life. As long as this situation of the 'two Marys' continues, the confusion will also persist and we shall continue to be challenged by the need to probe more deeply.

The theologian Kari Børreson has rejected Mary as a possible model for women because of this relationship between Christ and Mary at the doctrinal level. Mary, after all, represents mankind as the female and subordinate partner. A Mariology that is based on this principle is bound to legitimise traditional sexual relationships rather than help to liberate them.

In the symbolical language of bridegroom and bride, God and Israel or Christ and the Church, Mary stands for Israel and the community or *ecclesia*. In this typology, the female identification of the Church is in a relationship of subordination to the symbol of the leading male identification. In other words, the male is the leading principle, taking the initiative, whereas the female follows and also deviates from the way—in the Old Testament especially, she is the faithless whore.

It is here that the exclusive use of the symbolism of marriage by a hierarchically orientated Church theology has had a bad effect. There are many other images in the Bible expressing the relationship between God and his people and Christ and the community of believers. There are, for example, those of the vine and the people of God on the way. Each of these images calls another to mind, so that the mystery can be approached, but they cannot be traced back to each other, with the result that they relativise each other. What is more, they only apply to the ultimate dimension and cannot with impunity be applied to the changing relationships in society and the Church.

The relational symbols within which Mary is wrapped—the daughter of God the Father, the mother of the Son, the bride of the Holy Spirit—do not make it easier for us to understand what is essential in her figure. She is always presented to us as a relational or 'hyphen' being, in other words as someone who is always closely connected with someone else. Feminists object to this, because they are above all in search of themselves and want to go down to the roots of their existence. Mary cannot therefore be an identification figure for them. She cannot inspire them as long as she is only present in order to point (to Christ) and only exists in a symbolic relationship, as the receptive figure in contrast to the creative one.

Mary Daly has said that she would like to set the Christian symbol of the humble woman free from the stranglehold of the Christian patriarchate and separate the 'free-wheeling symbol' that Mary also is from the Church's teachings—the symbol of the universal goddess who has many names, but only one personality. A separation of this kind will not, of course, come about just by itself and so Mary Daly has distanced herself from the figure of Mary, convinced that she ultimately symbolises the violation of the goddess and therefore the defeat of a society that is more orientated towards the female.

3. NO IDEOLOGISATION OF THE PARTS PLAYED BY MAN AND WOMAN IN SALVATION

I am afraid that, if we continue to cling literally to the femininity of Mary and the masculinity of Jesus, neither women nor the community of the Church will move forward. But the fact remains that we are still thriving on the femininity of Mary and her humility and receptivity and on the need to preserve the difference between the parts played by the man Christ, who turned outwards, and the woman Mary, who turned inwards. According to Beinert two trinities have been constructed: the trinity Adam—Christ—the man, who all point to office in the Church, with the pope at the summit, and the trinity Eve—Mary—the woman, all of whom belong to the laity.

This way of playing with images is a great danger to life itself, because it closes the circle of images and does not allow any new references or comparisons to enter. It represents an idolisation of images, an attempt to make them absolute and therefore stereotypes. Women are bound to this procedure and even normalised by it. New and really evocative symbols can no longer be experienced. Christ and Mary themselves are both reduced to the level of rigid principles and Mary can no longer provide vital impulses making women critical. Statements such as 'The masculinity of Christ is essential for his work of salvation and in the same way the femininity of Mary is also essential as a symbol of the Church that is open to this event' (Hauke) are therefore misleading.

In the mystery of the incarnation, which was a divine and human event, two people were involved at the deepest level—the male person Jesus of Nazareth and the female person Mary of Nazareth. Because of this, the life-giving and evocative divine revelation at the centre of Christian faith should not be allowed to become ossified or destroyed by giving its form a meaning according to which the parts played by man and woman are now anthropologically and with regard to the structures of the Church firmly established, with the result that the woman cannot sacramentally mediate salvation.

4. THE SUBVERSIVE MAGNIFICAT

One of the few feminist theologians who has consistently concerned herself with the figure of Mary is Rosemary Radford Ruether. She has pointed out the many different ways in which the Church has made wrong use of Mary in order to keep women in their place. She has also pointed to the ambiguity of the symbol of Mary. At the same time, however, she has also examined whether it is possible for a 'liberation Mariology' to emerge.

In the liberation theology of Latin America, the *Magnificat* has been used as a source of inspiration in order to give concrete form to the messianic reality and structural relationships. Feminist theologians have consequently stressed that the words of this prophetic liberation canticle are expressed by a woman. In his *Marialis Cultus* of 1974, Pope Paul VI explicitly mentioned this connection (although he did not draw any clear conclusions from it). Ruether, on the other hand, has said quite plainly that a Mariology interpreted in the light of the *Magnificat* can form an important link between feminist and liberation theologies. This clearly introduces a stick of dynamite into a building that has so far housed a traditional holy image and Ruether insists that those who are interested in feminist and in liberation theology should let that stick of dynamite explode and blow away the outer covering of the image.

When Mary visits her cousin Elizabeth, she does not become enraptured because she is pregnant. On the contrary, she glorifies God's liberating action precisely because she is herself the liberated Israel: those of low degree who are exalted. Her *Magnificat* is, at it were, a prelude in radical, subversive language to Luke's Sermon on the Plain and the opening address of Jesus in Luke 4. In other words, Jesus' message is first and foremost intended for all those marginalised people who are summed up in the insignificant woman, Mary. Because of her faithfulness and her belief in the Messiah, she is the best possible personification of the Church as the messianic Israel, but only when this image is viewed quite radically and in its most profound consequences, that is, as pointing to a self-emptying and loss of power and a transformation of self into service. God emptied himself and became service in Christ and Christ emptied himself to liberate his people. In the same way, Mary's task was to continue God's liberating activity in the world. The last shall be first and those who rule must, on their way to the kingdom, join the ranks of the poor, whose head and example is Mary. That is Rosemary Ruether's message concerning Mary.

5. THE TASK OF FEMINIST THEOLOGY

At the beginning of this article, I made it clear that one of my main reasons for continuing to be concerned with the figure of Mary is because I do not want feminist theology simply to become a reactive theology that throws away everything that does not please it in (justifiable) anger and reaction to a negative history that has come about as the result of a misuse of power in the Church. Anyone who wants to continue to take Israel and the gospels as his or her starting-point has to do much more than simply throw away. It is necessary to examine very critically the origins of history, language and imagery and to look searchingly at the constantly changing context in order to analyse what is contingent and what is essential, what is revealed and what has in fact to be cleared away like silt.

(a) A Relativisation of Motherhood

I am firmly of the opinion that, although Mary's motherhood has been of fundamental importance, it cannot be used to fix women in a pattern of motherhood. Even in the gospels themselves, it is clear that physical motherhood is relativised by Jesus, who, as we have seen above, emphasises the *familia Dei* in his proclamation: 'Blessed are those who hear the word of God and keep it!' (Luke 11:28). Bearing and giving birth to a child are not in themselves called blessed—it is a question of following Christ, breaking, if necessary, bonds that bind too tightly.

What is unique in the case of Mary is that 'hearing and keeping the word of God' went together with motherhoood and were even the preconditions for it. The tragedy is that her *Fiat* has been presented by a male dominated Church as a diffident and passive reaction to the overwhelming Word. This tells us a great deal about the interpreters! In fact, Mary gave her consent freely and actively as an autonomous person who was, in faith, receptive and open to salvation from God and who responded to that offer. If we want to speak of dependence, then we have to say that God made himself dependent on man, who was receptive to God.

This attitude of positive and creative receptivity is the best possible attitude of faith. It is summarised in the phrase 'hearing and keeping the word of God' and this is a precondition for every believer, but, in our male dominated Church, especially for every male believer. The same, of course, applies to society in general. This attitude also provides a point of departure for a self-emptying leading to a loss of power.

Mariology has, of course, become distorted in its development and this, according to Tavard, is the result of an anomaly on the part of man, who has neglected this receptivity. The all-embracing fixing of the sexes, which goes together with a division over the structures of society, can only be satisfactorily explained on the basis of an attitude towards power which is threatened by any real change.

I have written elsewhere about the *Magnificat*, but what again and again strikes me so forcibly in it is that it occurs in the context of a meeting between two women, both of them playing a part in the history of salvation and both pregnant with prophetic life, and that the spark of the Spirit leaps across! Elizabeth is also raised up above herself and the child moves in her womb. All this provides Mary with the climate for her prophetic vision.

(b) A Critically Feministic Explanation of Scripture

The principal task of a feminist theology is, in my opinion, to interpret Scripture creatively and in particular the dominant images found in Scripture in situations such as these. This means in the first place clearing away the rubbish that has accumulated, asking iconoclastic questions and laying dynamite. The dynamite is not to blow away the roots of divine revelation or the essential truth of the liberating message of the gospel. It is there to destroy the rigid structures of the Church and of traditional Christian thinking that obscure that revelation and therefore make people forsake Christianity.

This prophetism can only be fruitful and salutary if we preserve a balance between the *Fiat* and the *Magnificat*, in other words, if our feminist protest does not remain a closed ideology, but is open and accessible to the work of the Holy Spirit. An open feminist protest may then become authentic prophetism.

If women are inspired by the Magnificat, men can at the same time become more conscious of the exemplary attitude of faith expressed in Mary's *Fiat* and make this a reality by emptying themselves of their dictates. *Fiat* is not serving others condescendingly and benevolently stooping down to help the poor. It is rather trusting in what cannot be seen and measured in the poor, the silent and the marginalised and suffering people of the world. It hardly needs to be said that 'male or female' no longer exists in the reality of God's revelation (see Gal. 3:28) and that we are all one in Christ. But this is not yet a reality and we must all learn how to advance towards it.

(c) Overcoming Patriarchal One-sidedness

Andrew Greeley has provided a very interesting account of a search for the significance of Mary in his book *The Mary Myth; on the Femininity of God*. He sees Mary as a symbol for the female aspects of God and this quest must undoubtedly have made him, as a man with poetic sensitivity to metaphorical language and symbolism, more deeply aware of his own *anima*. At the same time, however, it is not a liberating book with regard to women, because he works with familiar and traditional symbols and, although these provide him with a number of surprising revelations, they are not liberating for women.

Is Mary really an expression of the female aspects of God and is she the female face of the Church? Is Mary a female person who played a unique part in the history of salvation because of her share in the incarnation of Christ and who was transformed into a prophetess and an interpreter of God's salvation, thus realising that to which we are all called. Was she filled with the divine Spirit, sanctified and deified?

At present, I am inclined to accept the last possibility, that of deification, but I have not yet been able to solve the problems involved in it. A Mariology of liberation certainly helps us from the point of view of Scripture, but it does not bring us any closer to the deepest levels of the human soul. At the root of the very ambivalent attitude that has made the veneration of Mary so ambiguous throughout the history of the Church is this remarkable fact: the Catholic Church has, in Mary, certainly drawn attention to the female aspect that has for centuries been oppressed in the patriarchate, but it has at the same time also neglected its content of revelation and denied the divine element that has throughout history been experienced by men and women in this female aspect.

It is very important, then, for feminist theologians to concern themselves more with cultures preceding the patriarchate, since it is in those cultures that the primordial dimension is symbolised by the goddess. It has, for example, already been ascertained that the Church's dogmas concerning Mary are quite closely connected with the great visions and images of the early religions, but that the significance of those visions are drastically changed. To give but one example, the dogma of Mary's virginity is connected with the very early mystery of the great goddess who was a virgin. The difference, however, is that, in the latter, 'virgin' meant 'independent' or perhaps 'self-contained', but not disregarding one's own sexuality. As far as her own fertility was concerned, the ancient goddess was not dependent on a man. Her fertility was rooted in herself.

In the Christian veneration of Mary, virginity is originally a cultic aspect and it signifies that she was quite open to the transcendent element, but renounced any sexual relationship. Despite the fact that there is a fundamental change of meaning in the latter, there was in the course of time a narrowing down, so that it became exclusively moral and ascetic. This impressed itself firmly and permanently on the veneration of Mary and further on sexual experience.

Another example is to be found in the connection between Mary and the moon goddess, that ancient female image of the rise and fall of the tides, of growth, fullness and decrease and of light and dark. Very early in human history, the division into four times seven days in the lunar cycle was connected with the female monthly cycle, which was regarded as a primordial image of the constant renewal of life and death, as the primordial unity of birth and death and as the origin of all life and of fertility (Drewermann). It is therefore hardly surprising that, throughout the whole history of the veneration of Mary, married women have prayed to her for fertility and that she has been regarded as a powerful advocate 'at the hour of our death'.

Closely connected with a need to improve our understanding of the significance of these ancient images and myths is a similar need to know more about religious and depth-psychology, so that we can really discover unconscious human needs and longings. Everything would seem to indicate that we are in the West in search of the soul that we have lost or suppressed, the *anima* that integrates the transcendent dimension into our existence. As long as female corporeality, eroticism and sexuality are seen in theology and Mariology as a threat to man that may ensnare him and are consequently stigmatised, the female aspect will inevitably be regarded with anxiety and rationalised as dangerous and seductive.

Drewermann has pointed out that God expresses himself in Mariology in 'primordial scenes' and, if we explore these at a profound level, we may be able to build a dam to defend ourselves against the violence and *destructiveness of a paternal world* in which power, achievement and rationality are central and have operated in such a one-sided and distorting way that they have made religion itself atheistic. *It is only when the Church is bold enough to look at every aspect of the 'great mother' that full justice will be done to women and a sound Mariology will be able to have a salutary effect on women as well as on men.*

Translated by David Smith

Notes

1. The following books and articles have been consulted: Wolfgang Beinert 'Maria und die Frauenfrage' *Stimmen der Zeit* 108 (1983) 1, 31-45; Leonardo Boff *Ave Maria–Das Weibliche und der heilige Geist* (Düsseldorf 1982); K. E. Børreson 'Männlich—Wieblich: Eine Theologiekritik' *Una Sancta* 35 (1980) 4, 325-334; Raymond E. Brown *Crisis Facing the Church* (London and New York 1975) pp. 84-108; id. *Mary in the New Testament* (Philadelphia and New York 1978); Mary Daly *Beyond God the Father–Towards a Philosophy of Women's Liberation* (Boston 1973); id. *Gynecology—The Meta-ethics of Radical Feminism* (Boston 1978); Eugen Drewermann 'Die Frage nach Maria im religionswissenschäftlichen Horizont' *Zeitschrift für Missions—und Religionswissenschaft* 66 (1982) 2, 96-117; Andrew Greeley *The Mary Myth* (New York 1977); René Laurentin 'Marie et l'anthropologie chrétienne de la femme' *Nouvelle Revue Théologique* (1967) 5, 485-515; Robert Mahoney 'Die Mutter Jesu im Neuen Testament'; Gerhard Dautzenberg e. a. *Die Frau im Urchristentum* (Freiburg 1983) pp. 92-116; Heribert Mühlen 'New Directions in Mariology' *Theology Digest* 24 (1976) 286-293; Alois Müller *Glaubensrede über die Mutter Jesu* (Mainz 1980); Carol Ochs *Behind the Sex of God* (Boston 1977) pp. 68-82; Wolfhart Pannenberg *Grundzüge der Christologie* (Gütersloh 1964) pp. 140-150; Rosemary Radford Ruether 'Mistress of Heaven: The Meaning of Mariology' *New Women New Earth* (New York 1975) pp. 36-62; id. *Is There a Liberation Mariology?* (manuscript); Paul Schmidt *Maria Modell der neuen Frau* (Krevelaer 1974); George H. Tavard *Women in Christian Tradition* (London and Notre Dame 1973); Marina Warner *Alone of All Her Sex—The Myth and Cult of the Virgin Mary* (London 1976).

Maria Kassel

Mary and the Human Psyche considered in the Light of Depth Psychology

1. MARY, ARCHETYPE OF THE FEMININE

'MARY I SEE you sweetly portrayed in a thousand images': this act of homage by the romantic writer Novalis brings out the central point about the veneration of Mary in the Roman Catholic tradition. Mary is honoured in the widest variety of images, under a variety of titles, with the contrasting mentalities of north and south, at shrines throughout the univeral Church; yet in all the images there shines out the image of the one person, and they can be recognised as expressions of the single archetype 'Mary'.[1] But this does not represent simply the biblical portrait of the historical mother of Jesus: to a much greater extent it reflects fundamental psychological dispositions of a universally human and not genuinely Christian kind.

This can be recognised in the two characteristics that above all are applied to 'Mary' in dogmatic theology and are also rooted in Marian veneration: virgin, and mother of God. Both attributes can be found in the mythologies of many nations as attributes of female divinities. It does not seem by accident that the dogma of Mary as the one who gave birth to God (*theotókos*) was proclaimed in AD 431 at Ephesus, the city of Artemis, the great mother goddess.[2] The fact that these attributes were in the Christian tradition linked ever more firmly with the woman from Nazareth raises the question whether this does not mean that a primeval need for the female archetype prevailed in the Church as it had done in other religions, for example those of ancient Egypt and Babylon.

What is decisive is not whether we are dealing with the image of a goddess or not. What is important for the analogy between the Christian symbol of the virgin mother of God and non-Christian images is in the first place the function of this archetype for the Church that included it in its life.

It is widely recognised today that archetypes[3] in the various religions represent processes of pscyhological differentiation and form the stages of the human race's development of self-awareness. Myths for the most part contain the deposit of archaic stages of the psychological process of becoming human (the phylogenetic aspect). Since, however, modern man's psyche includes the archaic phases (the collective unconscious) and the individual runs through them in his or her development (the ontogenetic aspect), the archetypes also have an important function in the period of rational enlightenment.[4]

In the various religions the archetypes are preserved, are solemnly handed on and are psychologically appropriated; and this happens, too, in the Christian tradition. With regard to 'Mary' the task stands out in this sector for the Catholic Church[5] of contributing to the archetype of the feminine becoming conscious and thus serving the process of man becoming himself.

The aim of this essay is to throw light from the point of view of depth psychology on some aspects of 'Mary's' archetypal function as the expression of important psychological processes. The first stage is to look at the traditional form of Marian veneration: the second considers the possible future function of 'Mary' as the impulse for women and men becoming more completely human. Two presuppositions underlie these considerations of mine. One is my own 'Marian' biography. 'Mary' has played an important role in my life, as in that of many Catholic women of my age. Through her emotions were stimulated that otherwise could often not have been experienced in the context of a traditionally Catholic process of socialisation. A large part of my knowledge about Marian piety thus derives from my unconsciously experienced relationship to 'Mary'. After a long intermediate phase of Marian abstinence I am now beginning consciously to discover 'Mary'.

The second presupposition is that Christian belief is considered here under its religious aspects on the basis of which, despite all the differences, it can be compared with other religions. The psychological structure of religious experience and behaviour is similar. It provides the basis for the analogy of the archetypes distributed among mankind at large. The psychological function possessed by 'Mary' in Christian tradition can be derived from the comparison of mythological representations.

2. THE POSSIBLE PSYCHOLOGICAL BACKGROUND FOR THE POSITION OF 'MARY' IN THE CATHOLIC TRADITION

(a) The archetype as representing psychological processes

As the virgin mother of God 'Mary' emphasises a particular stage of psychological development. The foundation of the archetypal image is the fundamental experience that all life, both psychologically and physically, derives from the female. This experience marks in evolution the awakening of consciousness in nature and the beginning of specifically human psychological functions. Mythologically this is expressed in the image of the 'Great Mother'. To the primeval experience the all-embracing feminine element—in the exteral world of nature and in man's inner world of the unconscious—appears as completely autonomous. Within itself it includes the masculine generative principle that is not yet recognised as such, and thus represents the as yet unconscious human totality.

Hence the archetypes of the feminine in the various religions also include the divine element—that which includes everything in itself. And the archetypal feminine is experienced as virginally maternal because it brings forth life from itself alone. But it also has the aspect of that which devours and destroys. Life and death, feeding and devouring are the mystery of the 'great mother', as mother nature takes back to her bosom all the life she has brought forth. Hence the feminine is associated with symbols of light and darkness.

The character of the archetypal feminine becomes conscious through differentiation from the totality of the unconscious; and finally what is differentiated stands in relation to it as the individual consciousness of the ego. Just as the feminine gives birth to all physical life, so the unconscious does to human awareness. Since as a new psychological function this is something other with regard to the unconscious feminine totality and stands in tension with it, mythologically it appears as the masculine principle.[6] Where the phallus is dominant, where female and male gods are related to each other, where both these principles are experienced in nature, there the archetypes shape the process of the emergence of the human ego.

Consciousness becoming personal, in other words the experience not of being swallowed up in a psychological collective but of being an individual with sharply delimited frontiers to his or her conscious ego, is presented mythically in the relationship 'great mother—son'. This archetype assimilates both the human polarity of feminine and masculine as well as the psychological principles of unconscious and conscious in their original differentiation. The tension that thus arises is from the start a source of conflict, for the still weak consciousness is always in danger of being absorbed once again by the primitive and powerful unconscious. Even the battle of the sexes and the masculine fear of the feminine would seem to have their counterparts in the fear of the conscious of being swallowed up in the unconscious.

In mythology the son of the 'great mother' frequently appears as a divine child. In him the 'lower' psychological powers (the unconscious) are joined with the 'higher' (the conscious) to become the archetype of the psychologically whole human being. In this the son's divine origin indicates the aim of becoming human and his human fate the way to be followed in achieving this. The son takes his origin from being separated off from the fundamental maternal material; he must withstand trials and sufferings and for the most part must pass through the transformations of death to a new life.

This process portrays the human ego's processes of psychological transformation up to the stage of conscious integration of all the fissiparous partial elements, the attainment of a wholeness of being that comes close to the divine. As the son of the 'great mother' the divine child denotes the unconscious, natural harmony of psychological existence. The death and rebirth the son undergoes in myths indicates the goal of conscious wholeness to be attained through suffering. Thus in mythology the virgin mother with the divine son embodies the psychological process of man becoming aware of himself. The origin of this archetype must be the collective experience that man as ego must work himself out of the embraces of the unconscious and that this is only possible through the means of sexual differentiation.

Now we must consider in what relationship 'Mary' could stand to the processes of the development of human awareness.

(b) The functions of the archetype 'Mary' in the traditional Catholic understanding

Since an archetype always expresses collective aspects of psychological processes, it is only the collective effects that can be considered in the context of a general analysis. It is possible that in the case of individuals the relationship to 'Mary' has produced effects other than those described here. But these could only be brought out by an individual analysis of a particular psychological biography. Here we are concerned with the effects of the image of 'Mary' that can be experienced in the context of the Church. In this we can distinguish functions that are constructive for psychological growth from those that are more questionable.

(i) Positive functions

With 'Mary' the significance of the feminine for human development has remained present in the Catholic Church. In a Church that early on was marked by the masculine consciousness and was squeezed into patriarchal structures, that is a positive factor. It meant that the masculine psyche never lost its link with its origin in the primeval feminine. In the course of the centuries the reference back to 'Mary' had a conservative rather than a stimulating effect on the development of the self; and yet the feminine always remained there as a reservoir of further creative possibilities.

'Mary' has also maintained the dimension of the unconscious as a present reality in the Catholic Church. When the masculine consciousness threatened to drift off into cold, arid and one-sided rationality, the cult of the 'great mother' provided the rich imagery of the unconscious as a counterweight and provided a warm focus of attraction for the emotions of the faithful. Hence it strikes me as no accident that in Germany a longing for 'Mary' is making itself felt once again. Psychological forces that have been pushed to one side are looking for expression in archetypal form. In an age when the suppressed feminine element and the unconscious side of the psyche are trying to be developed, 'Mary' provides a psychological basis for this. From this point of view the churches of the Reformation could be asked whether giving up the archetype 'Mary' did not mean a psychological impoverishment with regard to man's development towards wholeness.

Particularly for woman's development as a human being the symbol of 'Mary's' virginity is being (re-)discovered as liberating.[7] From the point of view both of sociology and of depth psychology, this symbol expresses woman's autonomy over against man. 'Mary' enables the contemporary feminine consciousness to connect up with the primeval emotion of self-sufficiency in the matriarchal stage of development.[8] 'Mary' can in this way help to make the transition from the feminine independence of the archetype to the individually and socially autonomous humanity of contemporary women.

(iii) Questionable functions

The Christian stamp given to the 'great mother' is marked in the Catholic tradition by two psychological tendencies that belong together: splitting and individualisation. The destructive aspect of the 'great mother' was split off from the image of 'Mary': 'Mary' remains merely the good, caring, consoling mother. The dark aspect is transferred to the figure of 'Eve' (Gen. 2-3), the 'mother of all living' (Gen. 3:20). In this way 'Eve' could help to ward off the fear of the (masculine) ego of being swallowed up.[9] The splitting off of this side from the single archetype then led, corresponding to the ego's growth of individual consciousness, to the (mis-)understanding of Eve as an individual woman.

In her, instead of the archetypal primeval mother, was seen the first in the series of human women. This meant a change in the structure of experience from something that was originally religious and existential to something ethical: Eve was made personally responsible for leading man astray into sin.[10] The archetypal aspect of Eve became swallowed up in the Christian unconscious and was projected on to real women. Since 'being led astray' to awareness by 'Eve' includes the awareness of sexual differentiation, woman's character of 'Eve' was seen in the sexual seduction of the man. This explains why the Fathers of the Church and Churchmen generally regarded woman as the gate whereby evil was able to invade mankind.[11]

'Mary' was defused by 'Eve' and could thus fulfil the masculine longing for security in the feminine without giving rise to anxiety or fear. And for women who were devalued and kept down 'Mary' could, in the words of the litany of Loreto, become the comfort of the afflicted. For all her children she could become the Madonna who sheltered them under her cloak.[12] In the case of 'Mary' a similar development is to be noted as in the case of 'Eve': the archetypal truth of the good virgin-mother who grants everything and brings everything about was ascribed to the historical Mary from Nazareth.

The process of turning an archetype into a historical individual was followed by the biological understanding of Mary's virgin motherhood. And just as the negative aspects of 'Eve' were projected on to actual women, so the good qualities of 'Mary' were held up to them as an example. As a result Mary's virginity gave rise to the devaluation of woman's sexuality and the high value placed on virginity as a state of life. The psychological misunderstanding involved in this development can be seen in the fact that women as historical and finite beings were expected to live out the 'eternal' archetype of the virgin 'great mother'. Woman's psychological development was thus confined to a considerable degree of lack of awareness coupled with a deficient development of the ego. The fact that women in the Catholic Church have for centuries subjected themselves to the images of 'Eve' and 'Mary' is probably connected with their weak ego-formation.

The son's ego-status is characteristic for the relationship of the masculine psyche to the feminine. When men see the feminine predominantly in the archetype of the 'great mother' and her son, it is to be expected that masculine development represents the stage in which the ego has laboriously extracted itself from being confined within the limits of the primitive feminine and, out of fear of being swallowed up by the unconscious once again, strives to lord it over everything feminine—over actual women, over emotional potentialities, over the productivity of the unconscious. In the phase when the consciousness of the ego has not yet reached maturity, the masculine psyche obviously tends to suppress the feminine because of the latter's original power.

In terms of depth psychology an increase in the honour paid to the 'great mother' points to this kind of condition of the masculine psyche. As long as this state of affairs remains unconscious, the fear of the masculine ego for the feminine is seen as something negative in women themselves, and then it is imagined to be right to keep them down. There is thus a direct relationship between the privileged representation of the feminine in the virgin 'great mother' with her son, an immature development of the ego, and women as an object of projection by the masculine psyche. At this point the question can also be raised of the extent to which socially relevant phenomena in the Catholic Church are connected with the representation of psychological development in the image of the 'great mother'—for example, celibacy turned into a law and the education of priests in all-male groups, the exclusion of women from official positions of decision-making, the preference given to the field of sexuality and reproduction for official Church statements, etc.

The question now has to be asked whether the archetype of 'Mary', with its capacity for new life, does not also offer assistance in furthering the process of Christians becoming more human.

3. THE POSSIBLE EFFECTS OF THE ARCHETYPE 'MARY' FOR THE PROCESS OF HUMAN SELF-REALISATION

(a) The significance of abstinence from 'Mary'

When I asked students of theology what role Mary had played in their religious education, I received the answer: 'None'. Normally these students are from traditionally Catholic homes. Possibly there is in Germany a generation of Catholics without any relationship to Mary. Does this phenomenon indicate a loss or a gain? From the point of view of depth psychology it seems to be ambivalent.

The repression of the significance of 'Mary' in favour of Christ[13] can be understood as the expression of a masculine consciousness that is becoming ever more one-sided in the Church. But abstinence from 'Mary' could also show that the archetype of the feminine can no longer be maintained in its projected condition because that would lead to complete psychological stagnation in the Church. The disappearance of 'Mary' would then be the regression of the feminine into the Church's collective unconscious, in the sense of a process of incubation. This state of affairs would show that the feminine was ressing towards becoming collectively conscious and realised in the Church.

As far as I can see we cannot yet tell whether this kind of regression will be creative, n other words whether it will lead to a progress in development. The significance of the emporary abstinence from 'Mary' cannot yet be read off from the mere re-emergence of the feminine archetype from the psychological depths. The new appearance can also indicate a danger if it is merely the 'return of what has been repressed' (in Freud's sense). In this case it would be a cyclic repetition of the myth of the virgin mother and would not possess the dynamic aim at a goal that is characteristic of the Christian message. The mere return of 'Mary' could mean that the Church with its masculine cast of mind is incapable of withdrawing its projections on to the feminine and of allowing the psychological energy of development that is tied up in these to lead to independent masculine and feminine consciousness in the Church. It is nevertheless conceivable— and to be hoped—that a renewed turning to 'Mary' will provide the stimulus for a total humanisation in the sphere of the Church.

(b) Impulses for further development

Looking at the future, the positive effects of the archetype 'Mary' can only be deduced from the aims achieved by previous stages in the development of man's consciousness. In these concluding remarks I am therefore concerned with a kind of utopian project that must be proved by being put into practice.

The psychological development represented in archetypes is characterised by progressive differentiation of the capacities of consciousness, centred in the functions of the ego. From this follows the process of distancing from the all-embracing, feminine, unconscious primitive foundation of psychological being. Differentiation and separation from the origin nevertheless appear as the way to new unity at a higher stage of consciousness. It embraces feminine and masculine, consciousness and the unconscious, represents as the self (Jung) a more comprehensive and deeper-rooted individuality than is possessed by the ego of consciousness. This aim of human self-realisation appears in archetypes in the image of God.[14] What consequences can be drawn from this for the functions in the future of the archetype of the virgin mother of God?

(i) *The develoment of the man*

The man can be given the impulse by the son-stage of ego-consciousness embodied in 'Mary' to grow beyond this stage. For this he needs a new relationship to the feminine and to the unconscious. He can find this by extracting the aspect of the 'anima' (Jung) from the 'great mother'.[15] If the masculine consciousness accepts and consciously shapes its origin from the primeval feminine, the 'great mother' will no longer unconsciously lord it over the masculine psyche. Rather the 'anima' becomes a counterpart and aid for the man's growth into humanity (see Gen. 2:20).

In this way the masculine psyche could be freed from the compulsion to project unconscious fear of the feminine as something negative on to actual women; a Church that has been deformed on masculine lines could do away with its fixation on sexuality; and woman could become man's partner within the Church's institutions. For this stage of development a fresh emphasis will have to be placed on 'Mary's' aspect of virgin. This means that understanding it in terms of sexual biology would have to give way to understanding it in terms of archetypes, in which what is emphasised is the independence of the feminine from the masculine. As long as the masculine psyche is trapped in conflict with the dominant feminine (the 'great mother') it can hardly reach the maturity of being psychologically human.

If the Church were to settle down permanently in this stage of self-realisation it would be like young people wanting to preserve their puberty through the whole of their life. In contrast to this the autonomously feminine element, the virgin aspect, that would be integrated into the masculine psyche as the 'anima', would be able to help the masculine element in the Church to develop towards complete humanity.

(ii) *The development of the woman*

Women, too, can be helped to reach their full humanity by the virgin aspect. The autonomy pre-ordained for the feminine in evolution—biologically as the bestower of life, psychologically as the unconscious—would have to be transformed by women into a conscious emergence of the ego. In this the woman does not need to cut herself off from her origin to the same extent as the man as the 'other' sex. But things are more difficult for her to the extent that she must accomplish the attainment of psychological consciousness from a socially inferior status and is impeded in this not only by her own unconscious inertia but also by the masculine psyche remaining stuck in immaturity.

Virginity in the archetype 'Mary' can thus be grasped as a challenge for both sexes to develop their own specific form of psychological independence. But feminine autonomy in the image of the virgin mother 'Mary' does not mean seclusion or the absence of relationships. In the Lucan infancy narrative the conception of the child saviour is rather ascribed to the human woman's receptivity for the divine spirit (Luke 2:35). In the language of archetypes this means the joining of the primeval feminine unconscious as the 'lower' element with the spirit as the 'higher' psychological principle to form a consciousness which is suitable for the complete human being.[16]

The new human being who is both healed and healer thus emerges from the joining of the feminine potentiality of the human psyche with the potentiality that comprises the conscious totality and is thus divine. The masculine ego-consciousness that separates itself off from the feminine cannot accomplish this generation. It can enter into the complete human being if it joins in realising its own feminine element. Against this background it can be understood that mirrored in the symbol of 'Mary's' virginal conception are both the autonomy of the feminine and its relationship with the totality of the psyche. Hence it is precisely the archetype of 'Mary', the virgin mother, that can make us aware of the goal of becoming human: the whole human being who grows together out of the contradictions of feminine and masculine, unconscious and conscious, earthly and divine.

To sum up, it can be said that consideration of the traditional symbol of the virgin mother of God 'Mary' from the point of view of depth psychology discloses creative aspects that show that Christians are not and do not have to be confined by this archetype to immature stages of being a man or a woman. Whether the discovery or rediscovery of 'Mary' in the Catholic Church leads to regression towards structures and roles that need psychologically to be surmounted, or whether it leads to a new phase of fuller humanity and thus in due course has a positive effect beyond the Church's limits, depends of course on the attitude of the Church's collective consciousness to this archetype.

Translated by Robert Nowell

Notes

1. Names are given in quotation marks when they refer not to the individual person but to the archetype.

2. For the significance of Artemis for Ephesus, see also Acts 19. For Mary as virgin and mother

of God see Catharina J. M. Halkes 'Eine "andere" Maria' in *Una Sancta* 32 (1977) 323-337. Halkes brings out Mary's function as symbol in distinction to her historical significance. Evidence from mythology cannot be adduced here in detail: readers are referred to the wealth of material in Erich Neumann *Ursprungsgeschichte des Bewusstseins* (Kindler-Taschenbücher, Geist und Psyche 2042/43 (Munich 1949), and particularly for the archetype of the feminine, his *Die Grosse Mutter. Der Archetype des Grossen Weiblichen* (Zürich 1956).

3. In the language of depth psychology archetype and symbol denote the same reality.

4. The conception of the archetypes that is made use of is derived from Carl Gustav Jung's theory of the collective unconscious and its archetypical structures which was developed from the comparison of imagery from mythology with that from the dreams of contemporary men and women. The theory applied to the biblical traditions is that to be found in Maria Kassel *Biblische Urbilder. Tiefenpsychologische Auslegung nach C. G. Jung* (Pfeiffer-Werkbücher Nr. 147) (Munich [2]1982), and my *Sei, der du werden sollst. Tiefenpsychologische Impulse aus der Bible* (Pfeiffer-Werkbücher Nr. 157) (Munich 1982).

5. The Orthodox Church's tradition of piety is not taken into consideration here, although it could be fruitful in view of its wealth of images.

6. Looked at in this way the masculine is the 'other sex' (Simone de Beauvoir) and compared with the feminine is secondary.

7. The credit for this is above all due to feminist theologians.

8. If in this study mention is made of matriarchy and the primitive feminine what is meant is the state of consciousness of the human psyche at the start of the process of phylogenesis. Whether a social form of matriarchy corresponded in any civilisation to the psychological form seems not to have been definitively settled as yet. From the point of view of depth psychology the question about the social transposition of matriarchal and patriarchal consciousness should be answered differently. The masculine consciousness to a certain extent presses outwards from nature to structures that differentiate themselves sharply from the all-embracing feminine by a one-sided stress on conscious capabilities. The consciously organised and rigid principles that follow from this with their fixed hierarchical arrangements of subordination and supremacy can more easily be transferred to the reality of society than the matriarchal consciousness that is still for the most part determined by the unconscious and is not strongly structured.

9. The fact that 'Eve' is the dark aspect excluded from 'Mary' is shown in many German Marian hymns in which we human beings appear as the sinful, banished, miserable children of 'Eve', alienated and living in exile.

10. From the point of view of depth psychology 'sin' means becoming conscious, separation from the primitive feminine. On this, see my interpretation of Gen. 2-3 in *Sei, der du werden sollst* (note 4 above), pp. 54ff.

11. The fact that the masculine psyche links the symbolism of becoming conscious with the sexual act is possibly connected with one aspect of the structure of the man's sexual experience. Penetration into the womb could activate the consciousness's primitive fear of being swallowed up by the primitive feminine unconscious and falling victim to the dark side of the 'great mother'. As long as this remains unconscious it becomes another black mark for woman.

12. During the bombing in the Second World War we used in my family to sing in the air-raid shelter the hymn *Maria breit den Mantel aus* about Mary spreading out her cloak as a protection for us to shelter under until all the storms had passed away. It did not change the real threat, merely our conscious perception with regard to this threat. Today this attitude seems to be like conjuring up the primeval paradisical condition of being contained in the feminine without fear or personal responsibility.

13. As is done by Vatican II's constitution on the Church in its eighth chapter. What was then judged as progress in its view of Mary can in retrospect also be seen as ambiguous.

14. Since man is a being in continuous evolution, his or her images of God are continually changing too. Onesidedly feminine or masculine images of God do not yet fully contain the goal of self-realisation. In the Christian tradition the perfection of the self is embodied in the form of

Christ. The gospels indicate that the historical Jesus was already experienced as a person in whom the conscious and the unconscious, the masculine and the feminine were integrated, characteristics that in the dogma of Jesus being the son of God have been formulated as the core of the Christian message. This insight is developed on the basis of the gospels by Hanna Wolff *Jesus der Mann. Die Gestalt Jesu in tiefenpsychologischer Sicht* (Stuttgart [3]1977) and to some extent in my two works cited in note 4 above.

15. 'Anima' denotes the man's psychologically feminine aspect, as 'animus' the woman's masculine aspect. In the world of archetypes the 'anima' is ambivalent: if it remains unconscious it does the man harm, but becoming conscious it leads him to the highest possible realisation of himself. The creation of Eve out of the side of Adam in Genesis 2 seems to me from the point of view of depth psychology to signify this first emergence of the 'anima' in the man's consciousness.

16. In myth the principle of the spirit often appears as wind, breath or bird. On the basis of the structure of the imagery used in telling it the account of the incarnation in Luke 2 contains an analogy to the creation of Adam in Genesis 2: Adam is made entirely of the earth (from below) but only becomes a living human being through the breath of God (from above). On this, see Hans Schär 'Das Weibliche in der Bibel—seine anthropologischen und mythologischen Aspekte' in *Krisis und Zukunft der Frau* ed. W. Bitter (Stuttgart 1962) pp. 225-237, especially p. 234. In the case of Adam and Christ we are dealing with stories of man's origin in the language of archetypes: these express something about the process of becoming man and about God's becoming man in this process.

Karl-Josef Kuschel

Mary and Literature

IF WE go to literature for insight into the meaning of the figure of Mary, we have to know what we are letting ourselves in for. We have to realise that in literature much can be expressed that theology and piety, liturgy and worship are often no longer aware of, that literature may speak freely and freshly about a reality that tracts, theological speculation and Church pronouncements about Mary often by-pass or even repress.

If we look at the figure of Mary in genuinely non-theological, non-ecclesiastical texts, we find that literature is a *critical corrective* of the traditional stereotyped language about Mary which has become sclerotic. We gain in reality and richness of language if we take literary texts as counter-models and alternatives to the language of theological pronouncements and liturgical prayer, a language which makes a new, untrammelled approach to the figure of Mary today so uncommonly difficult. We cannot go into this problem at length because space is limited here. What we will try to do here is to point out a number of basic themes to do with Mary in German language literary texts, mainly from the post-1945 period.[1]

1. IMAGE AND COUNTER-IMAGE: CRITICISM AND SATIRE OF MARY

Criticism of Mary in literary texts is a phenomenon of the history of literature in the twentieth century. Medieval literature was mainly concerned to 'deck the figure of Mary in a passionate abundance of images and allegorical brilliance'.[2] For Romantic poets like *Novalis* and *Eichendorff*[3] who concerned themselves most with the theme of Mary she was a universal symbol of eternal love, unearthly beauty, divine wisdom or—especially in Eichendorff's late work—religious comfort, heavenly grace and fulfilment of earthly longing—all this in the context of Church-approved devotion to Mary. The twentieth century, with the works of *Stefan George* and *Rainer Maria Rilke* no longer has this religious and ecclesiastical background to the theme of Mary.[4]

George and Rilke were not interested in Mary out of pious devotion to her, neither were they interested in dogmatic theology nor in historical exegesis; they approached her as poets, lyricists and aesthetes. Mary as a literary figure was a symbolic aesthetic reflection of the relation of the human being to the world and to art, a relation with which these writers were concerned in their art and in their view of themselves as artists. In Rilke (strongly linked, as with all artists, to the contemporary view of women), this was surrender and service, caring for and waiting on things, knowledge of the mysterious and being open to the divine, prayer and praising.

(a) Bertold Brecht

Criticism of Mary only starts in the expressionistic and post-expressionistic period. Here for the first time elements of social and political reality come into poems about Mary: Alfred Lichtenstein's parody of the aestheticising Mary poem à la Rilke: 'Kuno Kohn's Five Songs of Mary', Paul Zech's 'Sortiermädchen', Ernst Toller's striking Pietà poem 'Die Mauer der Erschossenen' written during the imprisonment of this Marxist-anarchist revolutionary (1919),[5] and above all *Bertold Brecht's* poem 'Maria' from his *Christmas Poems* 1922-26. He says about Mary:

> The night of her first birth had been
> cold. But later on
> she completely forgot
> the frost in the joists, the stove smoking,
> choking off the afterbirth towards morning.
> But above all she forgot the bitter shame
> of not being alone,
> which goes with being poor.
> Mainly because of this,
> later on it became a festival
> to which all came.
> The rough talk of the shepherds ceased.
> They became kings in the story later.
> The wind, which was very cold,
> became angels singing.[6]

Here nothing remains of the medieval or romantic hymn of praise; it is purposely avoided. A poem with such a bare title is already a *reaction against the effect of purely affirmative Marian lyrics*. There is no epithet from the arsenal of praises of Mary, no aestheticising exaggeration. On the contrary, the style relies on the naming of bare facts. The poem begins with a statement of fact. Thereafter it is brought to life by the (thematic) *discrepancy between what happened then and what became of it later*: the discrepancy between the Christian idyll, with which Bethlehem was clothed 'later on' and the historical reality, what actually happened: a woman—Mary was her name—gave birth to a child in wretched conditions.

There is no Madonna here, no mother of God and Queen of Heaven, but an actual historical woman who is having a baby for the first time. The criticism of the doctrine of Mary is in the poem's talk of 'choking off the afterbirth', the shame and the poverty, the shepherds and the cold. There is a critical tension between the historical event and what was made of it, image and counter-image.

(b) Günter Grass

After 1945 criticism of the theme of Mary takes its sharpest form in the early works of *Günter Grass*. In the *Tin Drum* he says: 'There are things in this world which—however holy they may be—cannot be left alone.' By means of *blasphemous satire* Günter Grass, who grew up in Catholic Danzig, creates a liberating distance from a pre-conciliar tawdry, trashy cult of Mary in popular piety, which had only been done before in the play *Love Council* (1895) by Oskar Panizza. Since Grass, *Marian satire* has become a significant theme in German prose. In the *Tin Drum*, he says of the hero Oskar Matzerath:

> I used not to be able to wait for a tram without thinking about the Virgin Mary. I called her lovely, happy, blessed, Virgin of Virgins, Mother of Mercy, you highly praised, worthy of all honour, you who bore, sweet mother, Virgin Mother, glorious Virgin, let me taste the sweetness of the name of Jesus, as you tasted it in your maternal heart, truly meet, right, fitting and for our salvation, Queen, blessed, blessed. For a while, when Mamma and I visited the Church of the Heart of Jesus each evening, the word blessed was so sweet and poisonous to me that I thanked Satan that he had overcome baptism in me and given me an antidote for it which enabled me to walk, blasphemous but upright over the flagstones of the Church of the Heart of Jesus.[7]

This text is significant not only because it satirically reflects the whole arsenal of Mariological hymns, handed down over the centuries also through literature, not only because the individual epithets are deployed here as pious set pieces in a language about Mary which has become almost sclerotic, but above all because this *satire is seen as an act of liberation*, which enables the hero to 'walk upright' in the face of the Church's oppressive linguistic power.

(c) Karin Struck

What Grass attempted at the end of the fifties by his critical reflections on Mary is attempted by younger writers today from the background of the women's movement. In *Karin Struck's* (b. 1947) novel *Die Mutter* (1977) we are shown the attitude of critical young women to the traditional picture of Mary with which they can only come to terms at an ironical distance. In this novel the chief character Nora criticises an *unerotic ideal of motherhood* (embodied in the figure of Mary):

> I find devotion to the mother of God a complete enigma. A friend tells me that he had long ago forgotten about a year's devotion to her in 1953, a Marian year, in his childhood. In the church, in front of the altar of the Lord, an extra altar had been set up for the mother of God, to which especially women went with their 'little moans'. Thus he has long ago turned his childhood experience into irony. . . . Mother love is supposed to be the mother Mary with the child Jesus. Mary has no erotic feeling when Jesus sucks at her breast. . . . Motherliness is always presented as sexlessness.[8]

2. MOTHER AND MADONNA: MARY AS ARCHETYPE OF THE FEMININE

(a) Resorting to the archetypal

Of course even Günter Grass's work does not only have satirical passages about Mary. In *Cat and Mouse* published in 1961 there are numerous references to the 'Virgin Mary' and the protagonist's excessive cult of Mary reveals the mythical-archetypal significance of the figure of Mary.[9] The ancient myth of the Magna Mater enters the field of German literary treatment of Mary with *Novalis*, at the latest, in his idea of a *unity of motherhood* (propounded in his novel *Heinrich von Ofterdingen*). Mary becomes an archetype of the feminine in literature. In the first half of this century this motif appears especially strongly in the works of *Herman Hesse* (particularly *Narziss und Goldmund* 1930) and *Alfred Döblin* (*Mary's Conception* 1911; *Flight from Heaven* 1920; *Polish*

H

Journey 1920). Hermann Hesse, a writer with a Protestant background who was interested in Indian mythology and Jungian depth psychology, writes characteristically:

> I allow myself my own cult and my own mythology of the Madonna. She stands in my temple beside Venus and Krishna. As a symbol of the soul, as an image of living, saving light swaying backwards and forwards between the poles of the world, between nature and spirit, and kindling the light of love, the Mother of God is for me the holiest form of all religions.[10]

(b) Heinrich Böll

After 1945 this mythical-archetypal tradition was taken up in particular by *Heinrich Böll*. The *Poem on the City of Cologne* (1968), this writer's home town, is characteristic. In fact which city is as appropriate as Cologne on the Rhine with its centuries-old pagan (Roman) and Christian history *to display the mythical ambivalence of the Madonna figure*?

> Listen in the waters
> you can hear her
> in labyrinths
> under the city
> over stones, shards, bones
> stumbles the Madonna
> behind Venus
> to convert her
> in vain
> in vain her Son behind Dionysis
> in vain Gereon behind Caesar
> mocking laughter
> listen in the waters
> you can hear it
>
> The dark mother
> unimproved by history
> stands filthy
> fair of face
> in labyrinths
> under the city
> she couples the Madonna
> to Dionysis
> reconciles the Son with Venus
> compels Gereon and Caesar
> to the great coalition
> she couples herself
> to all who are good money.[11]

This is a lyrical text, transparent in structure, with one theme running through it which achieves a fine effect by the narrowing of historical perspectives. Venus and Mary, the goddess of love and the mother 'goddess', Jesus and Dionysis, the 'god' of suffering and the god of pleasure, Gereon and Caesar, the martyr soldier and the soldier emperor, are archetypal figures of human behaviour and represent the *'eternal duality of pagan-Christian history'*. The first verse is about historical 'in vainness'. The 'stumbling' of the Madonna is an image of Christianity's attempt, which always fails, to overcome paganism, a process which takes place underground 'under the city' in the hidden 'labyrinth' and because it is 'in vain' only provokes mocking laughter. The reality of this city always mocks such an attempt.

For this city, the 'dark mother' has long ago found its own way of 'reconciling', 'coupling', the 'great coalition' (verse 2). The sexual metaphor ('coupling') and the pairing off of opposites from the first verse (Madonna with Dionysis, Jesus with Venus) is an expression of historical realism, which knows *no moral categories*. The text avoids making any moral judgment of what happens. Here the Madonna belongs in the colourful, chaotic, dirty, fascinating, unmoral-moral history of human reality, which mixes up mysticism and religion, cults and cultures, and goes on unstoppably, underground, which reconciles in practice what in theory can only exist in conflict.

Böll's outstanding literary treatment of the theme of the Madonna is to be found in his *Group portrait with Lady* (1971). For Leni Pfeiffer the principal character in this novel, both because of the numerous typological references to the figure of Mary and also the author's own testimony, must be regarded as a Madonna figure, although of course the type of the 'subversive Madonna'.[12] With this figure of a woman who is a type of the Madonna, this novel confronts the typically modern problem of the *secularisation of the holy* in literature which corresponds in Böll to a *sacralisation of the profane*. The American literary critic Ziolkowski is therefore right in saying: 'The parallel between Leni and the Virgin Mary not only means that holiness today may reveal itself in surprisingly new forms, but also that the Mother of God herself was perhaps "more human" than we are prepared to accept after centuries of Marian iconolatry.'[13]

3. POWER AND POWERLESSNESS: THE MARIAN DIALECTIC

Since *Goethe* made the theme of flight to Mary in prayer out of social or psychic oppression a subject for literature, in *Faust* ('Incline, O Lady rich in pain, your countenance graciously to my need'), the theme reappears in constantly new varieties in twentieth-century literary texts too. In literary texts the theme of Mary usually has a *social component*: Mary as a figure of the people, the 'little people', linked not with power and authority but with comfort, refuge, help in need. Brecht's and Toller's Prayers to Mary are impressive examples, as are Rilke's Poem-Cycle *Girl's Prayer to Mary*, Döblin's story 'Modern', Hesse's lyrical *Songs of Mary*,[14] and also Franz Werfel's novel about Mary *The Song of Bernadette* (1941), with which this Jewish author fulfilled a vow made about his successful flight from France to North America.

This social theme may be theologically and spiritually developed by Christian authors. It appears in *Gertrud von le Fort's* novel *The Magdeburg Wedding* (1941) in which the figure of Mary informs the Christian dialectic between defeat and victory, weakness and strength, death and life. In a Christendom torn to pieces by a bloody denominational war (the novel takes place during the Thirty Years' War), the suppression of beliefs by force is portrayed as the 'suppression' of Mary and simply wrong.

The dialectic symbolised in the crucified Christ and his suffering mother is also present where Christianity is practised in lowliness, where love is offered in the knowledge of defeat and collapse, where being a Christian carries the sign of the cross, and the *ecclesia triumphans* is given up for the sake of *ecclesia sub cruce*. In other words: the 'Marian dialectic' puts the stress wholly on *criticism of power and domination*. Of course its strength derives not from political analysis of power relations but from the spiritual alternative it offers in the spirit of Jesus and Mary against the powers of the day: Force, Aggression, Destruction.[15]

4. POLITICS AND MYTH: ATTEMPT AT A NEW SYNTHESIS

As well as in Gertrud von le Fort, other modern literature written from a Christian point of view takes a radically critical tone. The *Magnificat*, Mary's song in the gospel of Luke which sings of God's liberating action for the poor and hungry and God's overthrowing of the powerful and the rich, is used as a key text by the writers of our day in *a utopian view of Mary whose stress is on criticism of ruling powers*, e.g., *Walters Jens* and *Dorothee Sölle*.[16]

Characteristic of contemporary writing about Mary is the attempt to make a new synthesis between myth and politics, no longer setting the mythical and political dimensions of the figure of Mary against each other, as Hesse and Döblin did, but seeking a unity which will have power to change and set free. Much of this contemporary reflection on the ecclesiastical and social function of the figure of Mary, much of what has made possible the revaluation of this figure (liberation theology, women's movement) may be found in the passages devoted to the 'Madonna' by *Luise Rinser* in her most recent diary *Winterfrühling* (1982).

This writer grew up in Catholic Bavaria, she is involved in the struggle for renewal of the Church and theology following the Second Vatican Council, she has studied the place of women in traditional Catholic theology and the history of the Church and knows *the ambivalent effect that Mary has had on these*: 'the Church raised woman to be a Madonna (Virgin Mother) so that it would not have to raise actual women'.[17] However, rather than juggling with the Madonna figure in religious and psychoanalytic language, Luise Rinser is concerned above all to work out the universal significance of the Madonna symbol in Catholic thought.

In a work on texts of the passion story the 'Farewell Scene' between Jesus and Mary his mother, she says:

> In the gospel of John humanity received a mother . . . that is: with the death of Christ, the male element in the divinity retreats and the female is given significance. Mary as projection of the female in God. The enthroning of the Anima, as shown in the Apse Mosaic in the Church of Santa Maria Maggiore in Rome. Mary sits there, Mother, Woman, Sophia, the Female, beside Christ and is crowned by him. . . . The many representations of Mary as the Madonna with the protecting cloak. What a comforting picture: a universal power giving us maternal shelter.[18]

5. POLITICS AND UTOPIA: MARY AS A LIBERATION FIGURE

In the poem 'Und Maria' by the Swiss Protestant pastor and important poet *Kurt Marti*, many of the themes that we have seen singly in texts mentioned here are brought together. The strength of this text, the involvement of which with Mary is unexpected in a Protestant theologian, lies less in the originality of the individual ideas and more in their synthesis, whose basis is a definite *political hermeneutic of the story of Mary*. We may illustrate this by quoting some passages from the text which is 104 lines long, divided into six verses:

> 1. And Mary sang
>   to her unborn Son:
>   my soul magnifies the Lord
>   I rejoice in God my saviour
>   I: an unimportant woman. . . .

2. And Mary could hardly read
   and Mary could hardly write
   and Mary was not allowed to sing
   or speak in the Jewish House of Prayer
   where men serve the man-god

   that is why she sang
   to her oldest son
   that is why she sang
   to daughters to other sons
   of the great grace and her
   holy overthrowing . . .

5. later much later
   Mary looked
   in bewilderment at the altars
   on which she
   had been set
   and she believed
   there had been a change
   as she
   —the manifold mother—
   was highly praised
   as a maiden

   but most of all
   she was troubled
   by the blasphemous kneeling
   of potentates and officers
   against whom she had once sung
   full of hope

6. And Mary walked
   out of the pictures
   and climbed
   down from her altars . . .
   and she was
       burnt as a witch
       a million times over
       in a false god's honour
   and she was
       little Theresa
       and Rosa Luxembourg too
   and she was
       Simone Weil 'la vierge rouge'
       and witness to the absolute
   and she was
       the lion Madonna naked
       on the lion's back
       riding for her Indians
   and she was and she is
       many-bodied many-voiced
       the subversive hope
       of her song.[19]

As for other writers, the *Magnificat* is the starting point for a political-utopian view of Mary. Like Brecht, Marti begins with the historical and critical and then immediately looks at the historical person of Mary. She has become completely the 'simple woman of the people' whose 'song' is an expression of her inner freedom and salvation. The expressions 'men serve the man-god' and 'holy overthrowing' make the text's double attack clear from the beginning: Mary is for Marti *a figure of female emancipation* and of *liberation history in general*. Verses 3 and 4 take up the theme 'mother' which we first heard in the first verse with the allusion to her song to her 'unborn son'. In verse 5 we are shown, as in Brecht, the difference between real history and history as it is told. Verse 6 describes Mary taking action and also a process of *universalisation of the cause of Mary through history*. The thesis is: Mary is not alive in the pictures and on the altars where she is worshipped but everywhere where social and spiritual *liberation* takes place through women, where women introduce changes or become sacrifices to power and oppression.

The final lines in the form of a rondo take up the beginning of the poem again. The 'subversive hope' of the end corresponds with the 'holy overthrowing' of the beginning. Subversive hope is a variation of a theme of Heinrich Böll's. However, in contrast to Böll, and many other writers, here we have no reference to the mythology of the eternal woman, the great mother or first mother. On the contrary: *history* stands here in clear *opposition to myth*, history interpreted as change and not 'eternalising' of universal, archetypal basic structures.

Thus here Mary is not the eternal but the *particular woman* whose cause is of course an 'eternal theme' of world history: the advance of the process of awareness of freedom and justice among human beings. Thus and only thus Mary is a universal symbol for Marti: she stands for a cause which under many guises and with many interruptions persists to this day: the liberation of humanity through God, which began in Mary the mother and Jesus the Son.

Translated by Dinah Livingstone

Notes

1. The basis of this short article is my detailed work: *Maria in der deutschen Literatur des 20 Jahrhunderts* due to appear in the *Handbuch für Marienkunde* ed. W. Beinert and H. Petri in autumn 83/spring 84 from Verlag Pustet, Regensburg. See this work for a treatment in greater depth and also for the bibliography.

2. H. Fromm, article 'Mariendichtung' in *Reallexicon der deutschen Literaturgeschichte* ed. P. Merker, W. Stammler, 2nd ed. by W. Kohlschmidt, W. Mohr (Bern 1965) pp. 271-291. The quotation is to be found on p. 281.

3. See in Novalis esp. *Geistliche Lieder: Werke und Briefe* ed. A. Kelletat (Munich 1962) pp. 84-102; *Heinrich von Ofterding* Novel (Part I chap. 8). For J. v. Eichendorff see *Maria Sehnsucht* Neue Gesamtausgabe der Werke und Schriften I, ed. G. Baumann (Stuttgart 1958 (3) 1978), p. 273; *Das Marmorbild* Neue Gesamtausgabe I p. 343 *Kirchenlied* Neue Gesamtausgabe I pp. 282f.

4. For *S. George* see esp. the Mary Poems in his Poem Cycle: *Die Bücher der Hirten und Preisgedichte, der Sagen und Sänge und der Hängenden Gärten* (1895): Complete works vol. VIII (Berlin 1930). For *R. M. Rilke* see esp. *Gebete der Mädchen zur Maria* (1889): Collected works in 12 vols., I, ed. E. Zinn (Frankfurt/M 1976) pp. 182-190; *Alle in Einer* (1897): Collected Works II, pp. 665-681; *Himmelfahrt Mariae* Collected Works III, pp. 46f.

5. A. Lichtenstein *Die Fünf Marienlieder des Kuno Kohn: Lyrik des Expressionismus* ed. S. Vietta (Tübingen 1976) pp. 164-166; P. Zech *Sortiermädchen: Menschheitsdämmerung. Ein*

Dokument des Expressionismus ed. K. Pinthus (Hamburg 1959) pp. 55f; E. Toller *Die Mauer der Erschossenen. Pieta* (Stadelheim 1919): Collected Works II, ed. J. M. Spalek and W. Frühwald (Munich 1978) p. 314.

6. B. Brecht *Weihnachtsgedichte* Collected Works VIII (Frankfurt/M 1967) pp. 122-125.

7. G. Grass *Die Blechtrommel* Novel (1959). Paperback edition (Frankfurt/M 1962) pp. 111f.

8. K. Struck *Die Mutter* (1975) Paperback ed. (Frankfurt/M 1980) pp. 106 and 114.

9. See the interpretation of Th. Xielkowski *Fictional Transfigurations of Jesus* (Princeton 1972) pp. 238-250.

10. H. Hesse *Madonnenfest im Tessin* (1924): Collected Works, VI (Frankfurt/M 1970) pp. 332-337. The quotation is to be found on p. 334.

11. H. Böll *Köln 1* (1968); Works, VI, ed. B. Balzer (Cologne 1978) p. 23.

12. See *Die subversive Madonna Ein Schlüssel zum Werk Heinrich Bölls* ed. R. Matthaei (Cologne 1975).

13. Th. Xielkowski *Typologie und 'Einfache Form' in 'Gruppenbild mit Dame': Subversive Madonna* p. 137.

14. A. Döblin *Modern. Ein Bild der Gegenwart: Jagende Rosse. Der Schwarze Vorhang und andere frühe Erzählwerke* (Olten-Freiburg/Br. 1981); H. Hesse *Marienlieder* Poems in 2 vols. Paperback ed. (Frankfurt/M 1977) pp. 175f.

15. On a 'Marian theme' that brings out this dialectic see Th. Kampmann 'Das marianische Motiv in der christlichen Gegenwartsdichtung' *Theologie und Glaube* 47 (1957) 401-418.

16. W. Jens *Predigt zu Lk. 1: Assoziationen. Gedanken zu biblischen Texten* I ed. W. J. (Stuttgart 1978) pp. 17f; D. Sölle *Der Herr der Geschichte: Spiel doch das Lied von Brot und Rosen. Gedichte* (Berlin 1981) p. 8.

17. L. Rinser *Winterfrühling* (Frankfurt/M 1982) p. 226.

18. *Ibid.* p. 230.

19. Marti *Und Maria: Abendland.* Poems (Darmstadt-Neuwied 1980) pp. 41-44.

Contributors

KARI ELISABETH BØRRESEN, a Roman Catholic, was born in Oslo, Norway, in 1932. She was awarded the degree of *Magister artium* in the history of ideas in 1960, and of *Doctor philosophiae* in 1968, at the University of Oslo. She has studied and done research abroad, particularly in Paris and Rome. Her publications include *Subordination and Equivalence. The Nature and Role of Woman in Augustine and Thomas Aquinas* (revised edition Washington 1981), *Anthropologie médiévale et théologie mariale* (Oslo 1971), and a number of articles in the field of theological anthropology.

Her present post is research professor, Royal Norwegian Ministry of Cultural and Scientific Affairs. She has been visiting professor in the theology faculty of the Gregorian University, Rome (1977-79), the independent faculty of Protestant theology (ecumenical chair) in the University of Geneva (1981), and the Divinity School, Harvard University (1981-82). She has been a member of the Council of the International Association of Patristic Studies since 1979.

SCHALOM BEN-CHORIN was born in 1913 in Munich. After studying comparative religion there as a main subject he emigrated to Jerusalem in 1935. There he has been active fostering progressive Judaism in Israel and the dialogue between Christians and Jews. Among his main publications are: *Bruder Jesus* (1967), *Mutter Mirjam* (1971), *Zwiesprache mit Martin Buber* (1966), *Theologia Judaica* (1982).

VIRGIL ELIZONDO, PhD, STD, was born in San Antonio, Texas (USA), studied at the Ateneo University (Manila); at the East Asian Pastoral Institute (Manila); and at the Institut Catholique (Paris). Since 1971 he has been president of the Mexican American Cultural Center in San Antonio. He has published numerous books and articles and been on the editorial board of *Concilium*, *Catequesis Latino Americana* and of the *God is With Us* Catechetical Series (Sadlier Publishers, Inc., USA). He does much theological reflection with the grass-roots people in the poor neighbourhoods of the USA.

CATHARINA J. M. HALKES is a member of the theological faculty of the Catholic University of Nijmegen, where she teaches with a special emphasis on 'feminism and Christianity'. She was born in Vlaardingen in 1920. She studied Dutch language and literature together with the history of medieval philosophy at Leiden and later pastoral theology at Utrecht and Nijmegen. In 1970, she became a pastoral supervisor in the theological faculty and from 1977 onwards she has been teaching feminist theology. In addition to contributions to theological and other journals and symposia, she has published *Als vrouwen aan het woord komen—Aspecten van de feministische theologie* (Kampen 1977), which she edited together with Daan Buddingh, *Met Mirjam is het begonnen—Opstandige vrouwen op zoek naar hun geloof* (Kampen 1980) and *Op Water en Brood* (Baarn 1981), which she edited.

MARIA KASSEL was born in Frankenthal, West Germany, in 1931. She studied Catholic theology and German and for a long time taught in a *Gymnasium* (grammar school). Since 1964 she has been professor of religious education at the Catholic faculty of theology at Münster University and is concerned with the further education of religious education teachers and with adult education. She is particularly interested in the relations between theology and depth psychology with regard to the Bible and the training of teachers.

Her publications include: *Biblische Urbilder* (²1982); *Sei, der du werden sollst* (1982); *Religiöse Erfahrung in und mit Märchen* (Religions-pädagogische Beiträge 8/1981); 'Tiefenpsychologische Anmerkungen zur Persönlichkeit des Religionslehrers' in *Religionslehrer—Person und Beruf* ed. H. G. Heimbrock (1982).

KARL-JOSEF KUSCHEL was born in 1948. He studied German and theology at the universities of Bochum and Tübingen, and gained his doctorate in theology in 1977. Between 1973-81 he was academic assistant and since 1981 he has been academic adviser in the Institute for Ecumenical Research of the University of Tübingen and lecturer in the Catholic theological faculty. His publications include *Jesus in der deutschsprächigen Gegenwartsliteratur* (1978); *Hans Küng. Weg und Werk* (with H. Häring) (1978); *Heute noch knien? Über ein Bild von Edouard Manet* (1979); *Stellvertreter Christi? Der Papst in der zeitgenössischen Literatur* (1980); *Der andere Jesus. Ein Lesebuch moderner literarischer Texte* (1983).

JOHN MACKENZIE has written numerous books, including the following: *The Two-edged Sword: An Interpretation of the Old Testament* (1956); *Myths and Realities: Studies in Biblical Theology* (1962); *Dictionary of the Bible* (1965); *The Power and the Wisdom: An Interpretation of the New Testament* (1965); *Authority in the Church* (1966); *Vital Concepts of the Bible* (1967); *A Theology of the New Testament* (1974).

GOTTFRIED MARON was born in 1928 at Osterwieck-im-Harz, Germany. He studied theology in Göttingen and gained his doctorate in theology in 1956. Between 1963-65 he was official reporter of the Evangelical Church in Germany at Vatican II. In 1969 he became university lecturer at Erlangen, in 1973 professor of church history at the Church University in Berlin and in 1976 professor of church history and history of dogma at the University of Kiel. Since 1979 he has been president of the Evangelical Council. His publications include *Evangelischer Bericht vom Konzil*, II-IV *Session* (1964-66); *Kirche und Rechtfertigung. Eine kontrovers-theologische Untersuchung, ausgehend von den Texten des Il Vatikanischen Konzils* (1969); *Die römisch-katholische Kirche von 1870-1970* (1972); *Das gegenwärtige katholische Lutherbild* (1982). He has also made various contributions to the history of the age of the Reformation.

ELISABETH MOLTMANN-WENDEL, doctor of theology, is the author of a number of publications on women, theology and the Church. Her books on the subject are: *Menschenrechte für die Frau* (1974; 2nd and 3rd ed. under the title *Frauenbefreiung— biblische und theologische Arguments*, 1982); *Freiheit, Gleichheit, Schwesterlichkeit*, 3rd ed. (1982); *The Women around Jesus* (Eng. trans. London 1982); *Frau und Religion. Gotteserfahrungen im Patriarchat* (1983).

NIKOS A. NISSIOTIS was born in Athens in 1925. He gained a degree in theology at the theological faculty of the University of Athens, and did post-graduate studies at the theological faculties of the University of Zürich (1948-49) and Basel (1951-52) as well as at the Institut Supérieur de St Thomas d'Aquin in Louvain (1952-54). He became a doctor of the theological faculty of Athens in 1956, extraordinary professor in the same faculty in 1966 and ordinarius in 1969 of the chair of philosophy of religion. From 1958 to 1966 he was associate director of the Ecumenical Institute of Bossey near Geneva and from 1966 to 1974 director and professor of the Graduate School of Ecumenical Studies under the auspices of the University of Geneva. While serving at the Ecumenical Institute he was named by the World Council of Churches as one of the two permanent observers of the WCC at the II Vatican Council and attended fully three of its sessions. From 1967 to 1972 he served at the WCC as one of its associate general secretaries. A permanent member of the Joint Working Group between the Roman Catholic Church and the WCC right from its foundation (1965) till he left the staff of the WCC (1974) in order to settle permanently in Athens, where he is now full professor of the theological faculty.

His publications include *Existentialism and Christian Faith* (Athens 1956) (in Greek); *Prolegomena to the Theological Theory of Knowledge* (Athens 1965) (in Greek); *Philosophical Theology and Philosophy of Religion* (Athens 1966) (in Greek); *Die Ostliche Theologie im Oekumenischen Dialog* (Stuttgart 1969) (in German); and about 120 articles in French, English, German and Greek. He is at present also the Moderator of Faith and Order of the WCC, in which the Roman Catholic Church, exceptionally, participates officially along with the Protestant, Anglican and Orthodox Churches.

CONCILIUM

All back issues are still in print and available for sale. Orders should be sent to the publishers,

T. & T. CLARK LIMITED

36 George Street, Edinburgh EH2 2LQ, Scotland

GOD IS NEW EACH MOMENT

Edward Schillebeeckx

IN CONVERSATION WITH
HUUB OOSTERHUIS & PIET HOOGEVEEN

In response to the probing questions of his colleagues,
Edward Schillebeeckx provides a fascinating and compre-
hensible overview of his intellectual development and the
concrete implications of the major themes in his work. **GOD
IS NEW EACH MOMENT** permits an encounter with the flesh-
and-blood Schillebeeckx – a man whose thinking is driven
by his passionate concern to live a gospel Christianity that
is engaged with the great social, political, and intellectual
issues of the modern world. Clearly distilled are his ideas
about Jesus, the Scriptures, ministry and sacraments, the
future of the Church, the feminist movement, the liberation
of the poor. **GOD IS NEW EACH MOMENT** explores the sources
of Schillebeeckx' thought: the people, ideas, and experiences that have shaped his work.

144 pages   published in paperback

in the United States & Canada   in the United Kingdom
                                        T. & T. Clark, Ltd.

⊬SEABURY PRESS

Seabury Service Center · Somers, CT 06071

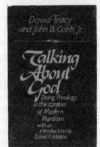

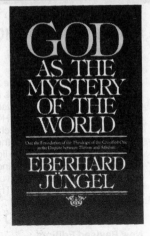
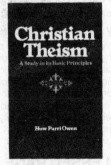